Conversation
At Midnight

BY

EDNA ST. VINCENT MILLAY

HARPER & BROTHERS *Publishers*

New York *and* London

MCMXXXVII

To
Arthur Davison Ficke
and
42 Commerce Street

To

Marietta

from

Mother

July 19, 1973

FOREWORD

THE manuscript of *Conversation at Midnight* was destroyed by fire about a year ago, when the Palms Hotel on Sanibel Island burned down.

Before coming north after a winter in Florida I had wished to visit the islands of Sanibel and Captiva, to look for seashells, of which there are some very fine ones to be found on these beaches.

I arrived at the Palms Hotel an hour or so before sunset, engaged a room, and had my luggage sent up. I did not go up to the room myself; I went out at once upon the beach to gather shells. Looking back up the beach a few minutes later, I saw the hotel in flames.

I began at once, of course, when I saw that there was no hope of saving my manuscript, to try to remember the lost poems. Under more favourable conditions, since I have a very good memory, I might have been able to recall the whole book,—if, for instance, a copy of it had been in existence somewhere, though at the moment unavailable; or if I had been required to recall it, not knowing that the only copy had been burnt. Conscious, however, that with the exception of a few of the poems which had been published in *Harper's Magazine* the preceding autumn, no line of the book existed anywhere except in my memory, if indeed there, I was handicapped by the strain under which I worked.

Conversation at Midnight as printed here is made up of poems from the first draft, remembered word for word; poems incompletely remembered, and reconstructed; and new poems written within the last year. The differences in metrical style, however, are an aspect of the book as first planned,—that is to say: the sonnets, for instance, do not belong exclusively to the first draft, and the free verse poems to the second. Among the excerpts from the book of which I spoke, published in *Harper's Magazine* several months before the fire, were such dissimilar poems as Merton's formal sonnet, "Lucas, Romantic Love is on the rocks," and Ricardo's free verse, "If you do not believe in God it is a good thing to believe in Communism." In the same way, among poems written recently, are three in such differing styles as Ricardo's lyric, "The family circumstance Is man's by choice"; his metrically free and freely rhymed "Since, however, the intelligible has failed us on every hand"; and Father Anselmo's sonnet, "If you live in the street called *Now*, in a house named *Here*."

It will seem at first glance to the reader that *Conversation at Midnight* is a narrative poem, interpersed with sections of dialogue. It would be better to consider it as dialogue throughout, to think of it in terms of a play, since there are not more than about thirty lines of descriptive narrative in the entire book, the narration for the most part consisting of such phrases as, "Said Merton"; "John said"; "Anselmo said."

There are several intentional breaks in the conversation, designed to help create the illusion of actual conversation, which often abruptly abandons one topic to take up another.

There are seven men in the room; sometimes their talk is general; sometimes they are divided into groups, discussing quite different matters. Frequently a person in one group will overhear a remark made by someone on the other side of the room, and will leave his own discussion to enter the other. If the reader will try to think of *Conversation at Midnight* in terms of the theatre, he will have no trouble, I think,

viii

with the disjointed passages which sometimes are the result of this.

Although I have given almost no directions for the physical behaviour of the characters, it is to be understood that Ricardo and his guests do not remain seated and motionless throughout the evening. They are smoking and drinking; Ricardo pushes a button to summon the butler; Metcalf enters with a tray of whiskey, soda and glasses; empties the ashtrays, puts some wood on the fire; Carl scribbles something on the back of an envelope; Pygmalion leans against the mantelpiece with a glass in his hand. At another moment they will all be seated but John, who stands by a table, slowly turning over a pile of etchings. When Anselmo rises, saying, "I think I'll play some Bach," Ricardo removes the bowl of flowers from the piano and opens the piano. Ricardo and his guests are all at ease, not stiffly seated each in a chair assigned to him.

For the convenience of the reader, I have divided the book into four parts,—to give him, as it were, three intermissions. This dividing of the material into sections has no meaning as far as the book itself is concerned; the conversation should be considered as proceeding without interruption from the first page to the last.

I have appended to the text of the book, together with the numbers of the pages on which they occur, certain lines from the text, usually but not always the opening lines, either of distinct poems or of distinct subjects under discussion.

The line quoted by Carl on page six is from a poem called *Joy*, by Robinson Jeffers. It is in the volume entitled *Roan Stallion, Tamar, and Other Poems*.

E. St. V. M.

New York
May, 1937.

THE CHARACTERS

(in the order in which they first speak)

MERTON: a stock-broker
JOHN: a painter
PYGMALION: a writer of short stories
CARL: a poet, a communist
ANSELMO: a Roman Catholic priest
RICARDO: at whose house the conversation takes place
LUCAS: a young man in the advertising business
METCALF: Ricardo's butler
FRANK: Merton's chauffeur

MERTON is a distinguished-looking man of sixty-eight, a stock-broker, very wealthy. He has travelled extensively, and collected some famous and valuable paintings. He does not care much for music, but loves poetry, of which in his opinion little has been written since Tennyson wrote *In Memoriam.* He is interested in the breeding and training of thoroughbreds, and owns a racing-stable. He has liked and admired Ricardo since the evening they first met, when Ricardo proceeded to outbid him at a private sale of old Dutch tiles. He is frequently a dinner-guest at Ricardo's house, but has long ago given up inviting Ricardo to dinner at his own house on Park Avenue, Ricardo having several times replied to such invitations by saying that he never does what he does not enjoy doing, and that he enjoys neither contract bridge nor the conversation of women. Merton is of

Protestant stock, and accompanies his wife to church. He is a conservative, and votes Republican.

JOHN is a painter, a man considered by his fellow-artists to be exceptionally gifted, but who is financially unsuccessful. He makes his living now by painting portraits. The best work he ever did is a painting of Merton; but Merton does not like the portrait, and it has never been shown. John is by nature a religious man, and is deeply troubled by the fact that he can find nothing in which he can whole-heartedly believe. He met Ricardo several years ago, when he came to the house in Tenth Street to request the loan for exhibition of one of his early paintings, which Ricardo had bought from the gallery at the close of John's first show. John is forty-five, thin and very tall. He is not much interested in politics, but votes, when not too disheartened to vote at all, Democrat.

The name PYGMALION is a nickname. Pygmalion is a writer of short stories for popular magazines, financially very successful. He is forty years old, good-looking, though not so slender as he would like to be, very well-dressed, extremely attractive to women, gay, thoroughly disillusioned, making the most out of life for himself, not bothering to vote at all.

CARL is forty-three, somewhat under medium height, physically agile and graceful, plays an excellent game of tennis; sometimes plays with Lucas, but is too fast for Lucas. Carl is a communist. He is a poet, and has published three volumes of poetry, two written before he was thirty-five, which both Merton and Ricardo greatly admired, one written recently, which Merton finds incomprehensible and infuriating, but which amuses and rather fascinates Ricardo. Carl and Ricardo first met several years ago on board the *Cabo Tortosa*, a cargo-boat bound from New York to Barcelona. They were the only passengers, and avoided each other for ten days. On the eleventh they got into an argument as to the difference between dolphins and porpoises, and for the remainder of the voyage talked unintermittently. Carl and Pygmalion were class-mates at Harvard.

FATHER ANSELMO is a Roman Catholic priest of the order of Franciscans. He is forty-five years old. Anselmo and Ricardo were born in the same village in northern Italy, and have been devoted friends since they were children. Except that his features are delicately cut and of extreme refinement, Anselmo's face is more sensuous than ascetic. He is an accomplished musician, a fine pianist. Whenever he works in the garden, which he delights to do, he remembers that he should wear gloves to protect his hands, but he never wears them.

RICARDO is forty-three years old. He is the son of an Italian petty nobleman and an American woman. Both his parents are dead. He has inherited from his mother, along with a considerable fortune, the house in Tenth Street in which his mother was born, a handsome estate in the country known as Black Hall, and a gentle and affectionate nature. He has inherited from his father a striking physical beauty and an aristocratic and subtle mind. He is a liberal, and an agnostic.

LUCAS is twenty-five, tall, blond and athletic-looking, hard-boiled and idealistic. He has beautiful clear grey eyes, and dark lashes of which his sisters are jealous. Lucas' father, who died suddenly of a heart-attack five years ago, leaving practically penniless a family that had considered itself very well-to-do, was a close friend of Merton. Lucas left Yale in his second year to go to work. With the help of Merton he got a job writing advertising copy; he is doing well at this, and beginning to make a little money. He lives with his mother and two younger sisters in Madison, New Jersey, coming in to New York to his work every morning by train. Just now he is staying in New York, in the apartment of a friend who has gone away for a month.

TIME: The present
PLACE: New York
SCENE: The drawing room of Ricardo's house, a fine old house in Tenth Street, just west of Fifth Avenue. It is the room of a wealthy and somewhat eccentric bachelor of considerable culture, who has furnished his quarters to his own liking. The room is at the same time luxurious and faintly shabby. It has a high, rather ornate ceiling. There is an open fire-place with a handsomely carved white marble mantel, surmounted by a huge mirror with an elaborate gilt frame. In the grate is burning a small fire of *piñon* wood from New Mexico. The curtains of the room are of crimson brocade and very heavy; they are now drawn across the windows. There are no books in the room; Ricardo's library is on the floor above. There is a piano, a long, plain black piano. There are three royal-blue *Sèvres* vases, two side by side on a round, somewhat littered table, one on the otherwise bare piano. All three contain white chrysanthemums.

There are several comfortable sofas and chairs, and a number of small tables for glasses and ash-trays. The room is brightly but not sharply lighted.

Dinner is over; Ricardo and his guests have had their coffee and liqueurs in the dining-room. They now enter the

xiv

drawing-room, all talking. Ricardo goes to the fire and stirs the *piñon* sticks, leaning forward to smell the fragrant smoke. Metcalf comes in with a tray of Scotch, Irish and Bourbon whiskies, soda and ice, two bottles of claret, and glasses. He puts the tray on a table near Ricardo, and goes out, closing the heavy sliding doors behind him.

CONVERSATION AT MIDNIGHT

Conversation
at
Midnight

ᔆ

"THAT was the year I killed five hundred quail,"
Said Merton. "Davis was down there, and he wasn't get-
ting a bird.
Well—'wasn't getting a bird'—of course he was; but he
wasn't shooting well.
'Dave,' I said to him, 'you can't kill birds with your safety
on.' You should have heard
Him swear. Well, I thought he was hopeless: he'd blaze away
Before he'd got his gun to his shoulder, or else he'd be so
slow
The birds would be well into the next county before he got
around to it. And today—
I don't know how he did it, but it's a fact—he's one of the
best shots I know. . . .
Can shoot circles around me. I tried to get him to carry his
gun the way
I do, cocked—yes, I always carry my gun cocked; but he
wouldn't; he said
It was dangerous. Well, I've never had an accident (knock
wood), not even a minor one.
And I can tell you there's such a thing as depending too
much on your safety and getting careless how you
handle your gun."

1

"And I can tell you," John said, "that the proper way to carry your gun is with the safety on, and to handle it as if it were cocked.
You've never had an accident, 'knock wood'; but there's plenty of time yet for you to have an accident, crawling through fences without breaking your gun, in spite of all the wood you've knocked."

"But dammit, I do break my gun going through fences!"

"Sometimes you do."

"By the way," said Pygmalion, "I'd like the address of that fellow you sent Bee-Balm to."

"Well, you're welcome to the address; but I wouldn't send my dog there to be trained, if I were you.
Bee came back slinking like a cur and full of fleas and thin as a rail;
And she won't stay in any better than she ever did; he's got too many dogs there—how can a man train sixty dogs? And you pay him five dollars a week to feed them and he feeds them once a month, if that—he ought to be in jail."

Pygmalion

Sam's got to go somewhere; he's terrible. He's got a good nose, and he'll hold his point; but the moment the bird's flushed
He's gone, and you can whistle your head off; and when he comes back if you give him a mild switching and make him lie down he doesn't learn a thing, he just acts crushed.

2

Dogs with that blood are bound to be difficult and high-
strung;
I know that trainers hate them. How old is he?

PYGMALION

He's two.

MERTON

Still young.

But I know how you feel. I'm getting sick myself of these
long-pedigreed stuck-up
Wilful brutes. If I can find myself a little mutt pup
That's cheerful and intelligent and obedient and holds her
tail all wrong,
I'll train her myself in two weeks, and you can have Caddis-
Fly's Phantom's Bee-Balm for a plagiarized song.

"It would seem," said Carl, "that the aristocracy is doomed
along more lines than one. . . .
Five dollars a week to feed a dog that may fail to find the
bird
It cost you five dollars to raise!—what risks you heroes
run."

MERTON

I'm going to quit raising pheasants if I don't have better
luck next year,
And buy young birds in the spring and let them out in the
fall.
That man I've got's no good. Conscientious, as far as I know.
But what do I hear

Yesterday?—a thing he should have told me months ago—
Suppose he didn't dare to—well, we'd been losing young birds
    by the dozen, and Andy shaking his head and saying he
    couldn't understand it and saying they must be lost in
    the grass,
And just about crying . . . and what do you suppose the
    trouble was?—
One day, just by accident, the truth was revealed. . . .

PYGMALION

Weasel?

MERTON

Weasel, hell!—we had a hawk in the rearing field!

PYGMALION

That's service. How'd *he* get in?

MERTON

Cheeky devil used to come and go
Through a slit at the top, where the wire had sagged from the
    snow.

PYGMALION

Didn't you have traps?

MERTON

    Well, we had. But my wife—God, I could have wrung
Her neck when I heard it—was afraid for the song-birds and
    used to keep 'em sprung.

PYGMALION

Well, if you're going to raise women, you might as well stop
    trying to raise
Anything else.

4

CARL

This sparrow-cuddling is just a craze.

Women don't care for song-birds; it's just fashionable; it's
    just a fad.

They go over their accounts with the cook, shave the expenses
    down,

Order the dinner, discharge the upstairs-maid,

Answer the invitations, try on the two-hundred dollar gown,

Then tip-toe back to Nature for a moment and with a smug
    smile

Stalk the horrified hen-bird about the garden;

Then sip some tomato-juice, lie down for a while,

And go to have their bottoms spanked by Elizabeth Arden.

The thing won't last. It's all due to the Charming Vista,

Which simply cries for a Bird-Bath, as a starving baby cries
    for food;

Soon it will be crying for an obelisk, or for Apollo's sister

Walking the dogs,—and the gold-finch will be jilted for good.

Then the Marie Antoinettes will roll their sleeves down and
    start going balmy

About Praxiteles . . . and the bird-baths will be sent to the
    Salvation Army.

ANSELMO

This "sparrow-cuddling," as you (and if I may say so, rather
    too prettily to support your derogation) term it, is far
    less dependent

On the arbitrary dicta of the landscape architect than you
    seem to conceive;

Nor will the Huntress, though carven from Carrara and her
    marble pack attendant,

So readily out-Phoebe the phoebe as you would have us be-
    lieve.

The Chinese gentleman who in the afternoon walks with se-
rene pleasure
Taking his canaries for an airing in their bamboo cage,
The captain of the cargo-ship with his parrakeet and his love-
birds will but in slight measure
Be influenced by what among the western ladies is "the rage."
And even among these western ladies there are bound to be
Always, I think, more than a few, for whom the summer dawn
Is lovely with a score or more of lively or nostalgic voices, as
it is for me,
Each with delight distinguished from each other one.
Here is a joy, it seems, you have not known:
The joy of knowing fifty song-birds by their note alone.

CARL

"Though joy is better than sorrow joy is not great." Why
shouldn't you
Be able to know fifty song-birds, or a hundred, if there are
that many, by their *cough*,
As you recognize a voice over the telephone? But what good
does it do?
Where does it get you? I can imagine your sitting and check-
ing off
On your fingers how many birds you can recognize by their
call, and feeling proud
For some obscure reason that you are so erudite in this feath-
erish way,—
But just how many hours should a well-educated and able-
bodied man be allowed
To sit with his eyes closed, saying to himself, "That's a red-
headed woodpecker. That's a Florida jay"?—

6

With the world so full of wretchedness and hunger, and every
    well-equipped body and brain
Needed as never before to keep our torturers from locking us
    into khaki again!

RICARDO

If the human apparatus can function at its best
Consistently and over an indefinite period without some hours
    of pleasure,
Some moments even of peace, of rest
From its own urgent problems and the problems of the frantic
    time,
Then why the shorter working-day?—
Merely to supply more men with work?—all work and no
    play,
However, being the desirable thing for each, if life could but
    be planned that way?
In that case how conspicuously wasteful that enforced and un-
    productive leisure
For which to some extent one had supposed your battle
    fought,—how unproductive save perhaps of restlessness
    and envy, possibly of crime.
As if a tree that bore sound fruit, but sparsely, should elect
To double its production, to bear twice as many apples, but
    all the apples specked!

CARL

Posies of sophistry, in a time of danger and despair,
To accompany the white orchids that the well-dressed
    woman will wear.

RICARDO

Why sophistry?

7

CARL

Because, as you very well know,

There are emergencies in which a prudent man will willingly forego

Not only his leisure but his coat and pants,—yet clothing under more orderly conditions might be considered highly desirable, and leisure also, even so.

MERTON

(to Pygmalion)

Now my wife's a good shot. But she can't seem to remember there's two barrels to a gun.

The last time I took her out (and it's going to be the last time) she got a fine partridge with the first shell, and damn near shot her foot off with the other one.

PYGMALION

Women don't do anything well except the things they were born to do, and not all of them all

Of those. Why is it that when the car ahead of you annoys you and acts in a way you don't understand,

That invariably out of the window ahead, and always a bit too late, so that you have to jam your brakes on, extends a small

Quite unconcerned bejewelled hand?

LUCAS

One of the best drivers I know is a girl,—but of course she's been driving since she was ten.

Good mechanic, too.

If there's a funny sound in the car she hears it before I do, and starts taking things apart—and, what's more—putting them together again.

Well, give my regards to the lady, some day just before
She gets stubborn about passing a flock of trucks that are
   dawdling along at sixty.

LUCAS

     Thanks. I'm not seeing her any more.

*   *   *

"Richard, you wrong the excellence of your mind,
That has no peer, perhaps, save in my own,
(Down, down, you rabble!—if you feel inclined
Worry the point, but in an undertone)
When you suggest that I establish Faith
As mistress in my decent bachelor head,
To frost with sugar the foul pill of Death,—
You wrong the excellence of your mind," John said.

"I never loved a woman in my life
Who had not something honest in her; curst
If I could take to bed, mistress or wife,
This wench of yours unless she won me first;
And crooked never won me,—could I think her
Straight, I should swallow her, hook, line and sinker."

"I," said Pygmalion, "on the other hand,
Am gifted with a most convenient knack:
Suppose I liked your figure—let that stand,
Just for the moment; no, I'll take that back—
Suppose I liked your painting, spent the night
Lauding it, heckling doubters, getting sore,
And someone said you slam the things I write . . .
I shouldn't like your painting any more.

Not that I've worked it out as fine as that
On purpose; as I told you, it's a gift;
I don't hand out cigars and, tit-for-tat,
You pull for me and I give you a lift;
No, if I hear you slam the things I do
I simply honestly lose my taste for you."

"I've got an aunt, who's neither worse nor better
Than other people's aunts; she has her ways,—
Disbuds her dahlias, occasionally writes a letter
To the *Times;* she's going to die one of these days.
And I'm the only heir; and if I hustle
And call on her, kiss her hand, drink up her drinks,"
John said, "—well, she's so rich she doesn't rustle
When she comes into a room, you know, she chinks.

And I could have a hell of a lot of fun
With ten—fifteen—whatever it is she's got;
And all I'd have to do is act like a son
While feeling like a nephew; and I'd rather not.
It's just not funny enough, it's not a good enough joke,
Drinking, 'Your health!' and thinking, 'I hope you choke.'"

"Incredulous God! Could I impersonate
John, do you think?"
Pygmalion screamed.
"Look at him, sitting there on his arse like a belted earl,
And not enough in his eight-year-old pockets to buy us a
    drink!

See here, my boy, *you* never had no aunt, you only *dreamed*
You had a aunt; it was just a *dream* you had!
(Get me?) Now stand right up and tell it to the jury . . .
Quick! before they all go mad!"

"I have got an aunt," John said; "what's more, I've got
A Heavenly Father—oh, you think that funny?
Well, I tell you if I work things right, as like as not
I'll come into Heaven, and anyway I'll come into money.
If believing's active, then believing ought to be easy
For a man in debt and a man afraid to die:
Love God and love your aunt, and don't be queasy
About accepting the benefits you incur thereby.

The trouble is, if left to myself, why, one day—
Who knows?—I might get fond of the poor old soul;
Trot her around to theatres, and on a Sunday
Trot her to church; love God, too, swallow it whole;
But there's something disingenuous, not quite hearty,
In taking up with God or your aunt when you're an interested
    party."

                *   *   *

Anselmo said,
"There are those to whom the key of *C* is red;
And the key of *F* the colour of dried blood; and the key of *E*
Clear blue.
I do not mean that the ivories themselves assume these col-
    ours, but that the quality of the key
Is red, or blue, or yellow, as the case may be
(Yellow is the key of *D*);
It may not be so for you;
It is so for me.

To those who have not heard the note of the bat, the bat
Swoops through the evening, dumb;
Yet the thin shriek of the bat has been distinctly heard by
    some.

You will admit, I suppose, at once the possession of five
Functioning senses; three of these are kept alive
By constant use; we hear, we feel and we see
With some precision; but that the senses of taste and smell
    will atrophy
In a comparatively short time, there are those who agree.

Pygmalion

Why should we smell or taste, except for protection,
The savourless food that for the most part we are content to
    consume?
Safe under Sanitary Conditions, under the Food and Drugs
    Act, under the inspection
Of the Board of Health, we open in a spotless room
A tin labelled "Soup," containing water, grease and grey
    leather slipper
Diced into cubes, and heat it, and eat it, and say,

"Well, the funniest thing happened—Who do you suppose
    called up today?"
Pouring scalding coffee, or, alas, pouring *Romaneé Conti*
In lusty gulps, over a palate smoked to a kipper.

RICARDO

In a thousand years, I should think, most of the people alive
Will have only three senses, and deny the possibility of five.

JOHN

I should not deny the possibility of the existence of five, or
    even eight
Senses, though I possessed only three.
Yet, if I, myself, cannot hear the voice of the bat, what has
    the bat
To say to me?

I'm a very limited person; I am unable to pick up pencils
With my toes, or wiggle my ears;
I know that there are people who can do these things, because
    I've seen them do it;
But I couldn't do them if I tried a million years.

LUCAS

You've learned to do a lot of things, though, in the last mil-
    lion years,
You never did before; for one thing, you've learned to fly.

JOHN

Not me! I've learned to be ashamed of being conservative and
    lacking courage, so I climb into the foul contraptions;
But the fiend who invented them was another guy.

13

LUCAS

Let me enlarge to you upon the comforts of modern trans-
continental flight.

JOHN

Comfort's cold comfort when your knee's knocked through
your neck some night.

MERTON

I've sailed above a billowy sea of cotton-batting clouds, and
it was all very sublime;
I've seen a rainbow shaped like a doughnut, and that was, too.
But I've worked it out, that I'd rather arrive late in Chicago
than in hell on time;
So I'm taking the sea-level route and leaving the air to you.

LUCAS

Well, some of our ancestors were the first that ever stepped
into a steam-boat,
Into a train, into a "horseless-carriage"; and some were not.
You feel at home aboard an ocean-liner, in a Pullman, in an
automobile, because they're familiar;
Still, a cabin in a ship that's on fire can get pretty darned hot;
A train can leave a trestle, a truck come down a slippery hill
in high;
The *Titanic* got rammed; you fellows are pretty fussy how
you die!
You're not so afraid of air-planes as afraid of the air.
Even if there'd never been a crash you wouldn't feel at home
up there.

PYGMALION

Why should we feel at home in the air?—See here, I can walk
My thirty miles, and I can swim a pretty powerful crawl;

But no matter how much you advertise, and how much you
    talk,—
The fact remains, I can hardly fly at all.

RICARDO

I always travel by air. I hate the smell of a train,
For one thing.

JOHN

         Yes. But what about the noise of a plane?
How can you stand that?

RICARDO

      Well . . . I do . . . somehow.

LUCAS

He has to stand it. Everything's noisy now.

PYGMALION

It's true. And I'm beginning to wonder what the hell
We buy that's half so precious as the stuff we sell.

JOHN

Exactly. Peace and Quiet poured down the sink,
In exchange for a houseful of "modern conveniences," and
    such an uproar you can't hear yourself think.

Every up-to-date gadget, every "labour-saving device,"——
We buy it, we have it installed as a matter of course;
Never think twice;
Let-in the Wooden Horse:
Noise and vibration; ticking and whacking and squealing;
House full of howling demons from the shaking floor to the
    hissing ceiling.
Yet "Onward!" Shout, "Onward!"—with the frayed nerves
    chewed between

The convenient oil-burning furnace and the labour-saving
 washing-machine.

Take the electric refrigerator, for instance. Take mine—I
 wish you would.

Delusions of grandeur, that's what it's got, all right;

Thinks it's the *Queen Mary*; when those engines start up I
 always say,

"Well, we're under weigh.

We'll soon be passing Ambrose Light."

JOHN

Take the vacuum-cleaner. I suppose it's easier on the mus-
 cles than wet tea-leaves and a broom.

But I tell you that when that monster begins to groan and
 howl, the sweat

Starts out on my forehead, and I can't get

Quick enough out of the room,

Out of the house!—out of the country, I would,

Except that it would do no good.

We're living in the Noise-Age. And there's another sense

We shall have sacrificed a thousand years hence—

The sense of hearing. Life will be

Feebly-to-feel, feebly-to-see;

Then gelatine . . . a gentle, tidal sleep,

Back to the amoeba, rocked in the cradle of the deep.

LUCAS

It depends on whether or not you're doing the housework,
 how you react

To these labour-saving devices; I'd hate to see my mother
 forced to choose

Between me and her vacuum-cleaner; I know darned well
 who'd lose.

JOHN

Even so, if we complained a little more, if we made a fuss,
Couldn't they muffle the thing?

LUCAS

Why should they? Most people love noise; they
go crazy when it's quiet. Who cares about us?

*   *   *

RICARDO

It was my habit of yore
To use several times daily a certain mouth-wash,
Because I liked it; it had a strong but agreeable taste.
But now that I read on every hand that it is an infallible
    (although temporary, mind you) cure
Of dandruff and halitosis,
Naturally, I no longer employ it.
Do they think I want to go to my engagements, smelling
Like a person who is putting up a gallant fight against dan-
    druff and halitosis?

LUCAS

They don't care about you. Who are you?—You're the ex-
    ception. Their concern is with the rule.
For whom do you think I write the red-hot, mother-love,
    body-odour, child-athlete, vitamines-C-and-D
Insufferable bilge that means bad-bread-and-worse-butter to
    me?
For the exception?—don't be a fool.
For the boobs, God bless 'em, and may their cringing tribe
    increase!

"Give us this day our daily slop," that's the earnest prayer
Of the advertisement-reader. And the daily release
Is designed to fill that need. Do you think I buy
The lousy stuff I am lyrical about from nine to five?—not I!
Unless of course, I have to; the good stuff is all but crowded
    out and you can hardly find it.
(Well, it stands to reason you can't put your money both into
    a product and behind it.)

Look here, supposing you had a new product and you wanted
    to get it on the market,
And you got a company to back you, how would they proceed?
First off, they'd round up a herd of lost and canny lads,
Like me, to write the ads.
Then the efficiency experts would tell you how many millions
    you'd have to bleed
To paste this tripe all over the Taj Mahal,
Mount Everest, the Vatican, what have you?—and in a little
    while
Everybody's lapping it up. And if there's one first-class in-
    gredient in it you waste it;
These boys that are backing you know a catchy thing when
    they see it and they'll put it over; but do you think
    they'd bother to taste it?
THE BEST—THE PUREST—THE CHEAPEST—BE-
TWEEN THE MISSISSIPPI AND THE NILE!!
But if you tell 'em it really is so, they'll give you a pitying
    smile.
Can you blame 'em?—They're smart! *Vox populi!* Just the
    bleating of a flock of sheep!
The kind that jumped fences for you before you had a better-
    advertised
Product to put you to sleep.

18

ANSELMO

It is advertising that has been the death of words.
The word "Personal" now on an envelope means "imper-
    sonal";
"Important," "unimportant."
"The Finest," "The Best," "The Purest"—what do they
    mean now?—
Something somebody wants to sell.

We are a nation of word-killers: *hero*, *veteran*, *tragedy*,—
Watch the great words go down.

CARL

The language grows like that.

ANSELMO

        At least, it changes.

RICARDO

Corruption, too, is a kind of development—it depends on the
    view-point. It depends on whether
You are the word, or the worm; and whose is the ultimate
    society.
To the buzzard under his shabby wings appraising the beach
    from above, the whip-ray
Till he be stranded and the land soldier-crabs have taken
    his eyes out
Has not achieved maturity.

This monosyllabic, meagre, stale, inflated, abused unlovely
    carcass
Of the great English tongue,
All English-speaking people
Clip or drawl, squeal, mumble, swallow, giggle, grunt—so sel-
    dom speak——

CARL

Has avoided death!—has adapted itself to the conditions
Of the changing time, and is their proper voice!

ANSELMO

It is the certain voice
Of an uncertain moment.

*   *   *

Thus are our altars polluted; nor may we flee. The walls are
    strong.
Such erudition as we have we must instantly turn
To practical account; we shall never again have time to learn.
For the barbarian has conquered—and our captors require of
    us a song.

Greek may not drown among the islands; it goes down,
But is caught in a net by trawlers, and set
To deciphering postcards from a modern Aegean town.
Nor may wounded Latin lie
Forgotten among the gutter-weeds and die:
It must limp in the Triumph; the lewd and snobbish time has
    use for those proud brows;
Thus Plato survives in a winked-at adjective; and Vergil
Is a name in the advertisement of a cultured dress-making
    house.

RICARDO

It might, of course, be remarked, that the wound in the Latin
    tongue
Was inflicted early, when the Christian Church was young ...

And whether it be preferable that the language of Propertius
    be put to work
As Altar-Boy to an alien faith, or as the clerk
Of a more temporal dominion,
While it may be to the devout a matter of knowledge, is to
    the layman
A matter of opinion.

CARL
(to Anselmo)

If your interest in learning is authentic, why not let these
    fellows speak
Each in his own language,—David in Hebrew, Jesus in Ara-
    maic; why not read the Epistles in the Greek?
Not at all, you're interested in the spell-binding power of a
    corrupt, a *lingua-franca* Latin chanted
In a burr so thick that if you were imploring Jupiter instead
    of Jesus, he wouldn't know what the hell you wanted!

MERTON
(to Anselmo)
Anselmo, if I wished to sin and thoroughly enjoy it,
I should join your Church.

Alas, I fear that since I was a child, and dreaded my father's
    wrath, and received my mother's pardon,
I have never known in its fulness the ecstasy of sin.

The Anglo-Saxon, four-square, Protestant man, not only
    strives
To be upright, but intends to be:
Perfection is not only the mark by which he steers, but the
    port where he means
To drop anchor.

This voluptuous sinning-and-forgiving, this quarrelling-and-
    making-up, is not a northern thing.
Your typical angular Protestant, setting out for Heaven,
Knows he has sinned, and prays that his sins be forgiven, not
    because,
Being man, he is sinful, but because he means to sin no more.
And he travels light; the taper and the ciborium are heavy;
    and he proposes to arrive
In Heaven on his own feet.
(An impious attitude, this, to Catholic ears.)

As for me, if I did not think I should some day crunch
The carrot before my nose, I should balk in earnest,
And sample the wayside weeds, from that moment on,
With a gourmet's respect.

Pygmalion

Unwavering hypocrisy, however, and a high ideal,
Make shift to keep us on the road.

Observe, for instance, the sheepy eyes of the next wolf
You see in a tuxedo, haranguing the lambs in the town-hall
Over a pitcher of water and under the Stars-and-Stripes;
He means what he says—why, yes, he does—look here,
"Abraham Lincoln!" that's what he says—doesn't he mean it?
"Our glorious country!" "Proud to be an American!" "Free
And equal!" "Fought and bled!" "This glorious flag!"

Weak eyes?—hell, no!—them's tears!

Do you think *he* thinks he's nothing but a mouth full of
    teeth?—
A larynx raw with lies and in need of a gargle?

A head full of soup?—A shirt full of sawdust, packed
Tight about a frozen heart?—Hell, no; he thinks
He's a darned fine guy!—and he means every promise he
    makes . . .
Means it as a *promise*, I mean. And that's just what I mean.

RICARDO

Hypocrisy is not to be despised. It is the pimp of Empire, but
    it presupposes
The existence in the community of a spiritual force for good,
    that must be courted and betrayed
Into connivance with evil, before the planned step can be
    made.

The overt act of aggression is more dashing to behold,
No doubt, but is impracticable where an articulate minority
Is against such acts. Aggression *there* must be sold
To the people under a softer name, for the opposing few
    speak well, and to speak well is to speak with authority.
The tyrant is less picturesque than in the old
Days; the high church-going hat crushes somewhat the wreath
    of roses.

Virtue, however, duped and tupped a thousand times by
    Wrong, remains the same,
Is ever virginal, smooths down her tumbled skirts in brood-
    ing anger, not in shame.

MERTON

I should prefer, I think, a little less nobility,
And a trifle more intelligence: if Virtue still
After so many Mickey Finns gulps down with such docility
Whatever is put to her lips, why, Virtue is an imbecile.

23

I agree. How can we have an ounce of respect, to say nothing
    of this pound of homage for—
How can we have any patience with—a mushy idealism like
    ours today?
Given an intelligent propaganda there's no limit to the num-
    ber of times a nation of pacifists will go to war.
This milk of human kindness is all *soupe au lait*.

John

Let the lupine human animal doff his sheepskin and come
    squarely out
For the crown of the planet on his pate, and a bloody knout
In his paw, and a crushed people—the things he really cares
    about.

Nobody need lie to us any more, we lie so to ourselves,—be-
    cause we can't bear it
That life should be so crass. The wolf in the bed no longer
    need bother
To fit himself out with a ruffled night-cap—certainly he
    needn't wear it—
No matter what he looks like, we tiptoe in with our cakes and
    cry, "Good-day, Grandmother!"

We believe what we are told, without question; Foul tells us,
    "I am Fair,"
And we believe him. "Don't shoot," says the crow in the
    cornfield; "I'm an albatross."
All that the darkey has to say to clear himself when he's sur-
    prised in the hen-house and the owner calls, "Who's
    there?"
Is, "Just us chickens, boss!"

24

ANSELMO
(to Merton)

To enter into a state of grace with the avowed purpose of
    more poignantly
Experiencing a lapse from grace, is of course impossible.
Our Lord was the victim, mind you, never the butt
Of the unperceiving world.
Faith will not enter even for a moment's time the disin-
    genuous heart, or be the tool of crafty enterprise.
Believing nothing, believing no longer even in yourself, your
    witticism
Gone sour on your tongue, before the serene and implacable
    beauty of the Mass,
Aware that in the presence of duplicity, because of you, the
    drama,
Sacred to the single-hearted all about you in that place, of
    the anguish suffered
For the redemption of the world by Jesus Christ their Lord,
    was being celebrated, shame
Would rise from your sickened breast into your hot cheek,
    and your repentance
Would precede your sin, and become, as like as not
Your initial act of Faith.

Strange, that a man who would not play with fire, will play
    with God!
You run grave risk, my friend, of being scorched by Faith.

*   *   *

CARL

I note with satisfaction, Anselmo, that in dealing with Merton you are as helpless as I.

The reason is this: that not only does he not respect, he actively distrusts, all things which money does not buy.

If Faith could be ordered by 'phone and delivered at the trade-entrance

He'd never be without a supply.

RICARDO

It is I who have faith, not John, and not you, Anselmo.

You are doubters both; you are for ever thrusting your fingers into the wounds.

The Church has built up a ritual so elaborate that the humble person,

Hurrying from Mass to market, has no time to doubt;

But you have time; Pascal had time; you all have time

Who have time to think.

Your Church is built upon a rock of doubt,—on three

Denials, and a dozen hearts of little faith.

What a man believes, he lives with quietly.

They build

No Church upon the daily rising of the sun, who howl not

With terror while the dragon eats the sun.

As for me, I am on a ship in mid-ocean; my vision extends outward

Like the spokes of a wheel, five miles in all directions to a round horizon;

And beyond that horizon is Mystery.

It has no face; it is not faceless; it is not conscious; it is not unconscious: it is Mystery.

I believe in the existence of that, the nature of whose existence
I cannot apprehend; for I am not equipped with the organ of
    apprehension
(Nor was ever a man so equipped)
In that dimension.

It is you, Anselmo, who are stiff-necked and arrogant, not I;
It is you who refuse to submit your will.
You cannot conceive that there might be that of which you
    cannot conceive; you are arrogant;
You endow all things with human attributes; you do not
    hesitate
To call the inconceivable "Father."
In vain do you strike your breast; in vain do you say
In a humble voice, *"Domine, non sum dignus";*
Whose arrogance knows no bounds; who have presumed to
    name
A mystery "God," and give it a bride and a child.

JOHN

It is not arrogance, Ricardo, it is utter
Terror and loneliness
That drives a man to address the Void as "Thou."
Man cannot breathe in an atmosphere that neither pities
    nor condemns.
This Life, this All-I-Have, my treasure,
Is it indeed in a dark unfathomed cave that it sends forth
    its purest ray serene?—
No ray, then, nullified by darkness, never seen?
It is against the nature of a man, it is against his deepest
    instinct to accept
That his articulate mouth in anguish to the earless Incon-
    ceivable speaks on and on,

That his tremendous, his important struggle to be kind, to
    be wise,
Is witnessed by no eyes,
And if he broke, or kept
With fortitude his proud and arduous vow
Not only does not matter here and now
But never mattered, nor ever will, and so he lives and dies.
And is not even *gone*
From where he never was, though there he lies.

Has not the elaborate cunning of this torture over and over
    stated
That though he is not loved, though he will never rise
Out of the grave, he has at least been hated?

RICARDO

Let us not hope to survive the other sheep, the other weasels;
    surely the wild boar
Is chiefest among swine, and should outlive us by a wide
    margin.

Let us not hope to survive the monkey and the beaver; these,
    too, have built bridges and dams.
The salmon, too, can mount the rivers; the eagle, too,
Can fly.

The bee and the ant, with their intricate, ordered societies—
    let us not hope to survive them.

Not so strong as the lion, nor so beautiful as the leaping
Antelope is man.

With what shall we pay our entrance into an exclusive
Paradise, from which the beaver and the ant are barred?
With a non-functioning excellence?—An atrophied
Superiority?—
With this vestigial mind?

O Reason, O ill-starred!
Our single talent! We have buried you in a mole's house,
    chuckling
That the mole was blind.

Let us abdicate now; let us disintegrate quietly here, con-
    vivially imbibing
The pleasanter poisons.

                    *   *   *

RICARDO
(to John)

Since, as for me, I have no hope, no haven,
No promise of welcome from water-front windows, from nar-
    rowed keen
Kind eyes above a knitted blue jersey,—
I shall hoist anchor laden above the Plimsoll with all my
    spoils.

Since neither our destination nor the tiny forthright Hail on
    our stern has any speech for history, the voyage alone
Being eloquent,
What pride shall we jettison?—Let us go under with all our
    disdains—let us go down with our treasure;

Since the voyage and the sea are all, since the name of the
    ship is
"*Unavailing.*"

ANSELMO
(*to John*)

If you live in the street called *Now*, in a house named *Here*—
If you live at number *Here North Now Street*, let us say,
Then immediate things, discomfort, sorrow, it is clear,
Are of first importance; you could feel no other way.
But if you pitch your tent each evening nearer the town
Of your true desire, and glimpse its gates less far,
Then you lay you down on nettles, you lay you down
With vipers, and you scarcely notice where you are.
The world is not relinquished; but the world assumes
Its proper place in that perspective, is not all;
Is harsh with envy, greed, assault,—or blooms
With friendship, courage, truth, is beautiful;
Yet is at best but an inn on a thoroughfare:
Provincial, one might call the mind contented there.

JOHN
(*aloud, but as if to himself*)

Belief, perhaps, is at the opposite pole
From thought; their functions cannot be combined;
Believing being the office of the soul,
As reasoning is the office of the mind.
The man who reads a book asks of the eye
Alone its service; he does not exact
Help from the ear as well; if he should cry,
"I do not hear it!—therefore it is no fact!"
When speaking of a book, we must confess
This man unbalanced; persisting, he would be

A source of pity, not unmixed with—yes—
Annoyance, to persons functioning properly.
Belief has its own logic; I divide
Apples by pears, when I set that fact aside.

RICARDO

All creatures, to survive,
Adapt themselves to the changing conditions under which
    they live;
If they can grow new faculties to meet the new
Necessity, they thrive;
Otherwise not; the inflexible organism, however much alive
Today, is tomorrow extinct. Man, until aware
Of God as a condition of his spiritual environment, would
    know no need of prayer.
Man, then, has not invented God; he has developed Faith,
To meet a God already there.

JOHN

What God is that?—the one you don't believe in?

RICARDO

Ah, you mistake me. I was giving Anselmo an argument.

ANSELMO

I thank you. *E ben trovato.* But I fear I cannot accept it; it
    is not a Catholic
Argument.

JOHN

    Why not? I was impressed by it. I could easily believe
In God along those lines. That seems a sensible
Theory to me, and a plausible explanation. It sounds like
    something
My intelligence could grasp.

Pygmalion

You'll land yourself in jail, John, yet, with that grasping
Intelligence of yours.

Ricardo

No room then, for my neat, compact, and as you see
Not unpersuasive little plea
For Faith, even in your saddle-bag, Anselmo, even at a pinch?

Anselmo

It is the Church itself, when it must gallop to the aid (and
you know this)
Of a man in his extremity,
That is thrust into the saddle-bag,—compressed, but not
distorted; and issues thence
Gigantic in the narrowest room.
The altar built in haste of a board across two barrels is, if
you like,
A make-shift altar; but the altar-stone
No bigger than a man's clasped hands, is not a make-shift
altar-stone. Christ does not need to clinch
Salvation by a sophistry.

John

     Even so, must a man's approach
To orthodoxy in itself be orthodox?
Before he even learns to crawl
In the right direction, is he chidden for the way he walks?
I don't get that at all.

Anselmo

Faith does not require the existence of an added sense above
man's normal five,

Nor of a specific and distinct new faculty evolved
To cope with an existing spiritual environment of which one
    is suddenly aware;
We cannot *contrive*
To believe. Yet by an act of Reason the questioning mind,
Unlighted save by Reason, reviewing its own darkness and
    considering if light be desirable, suddenly may find
Light shed upon all, the world where he stumbled lighted, and
    the path before him lighted;
And the shadowy looming bulks of terror and despair
Chastened each into its proper outline and dimension, and
    resolved
Into a trick of shadows, something only in the darkness there.
Now are all things seen clearly; now is the unclouded eye
Perceptive, now is the whole intelligence a thousand-fold
    enhanced,
Enabled thus to witness, and to receive;
Now does the sharpened ear
Unstraining, hark and hear.
The Divine Gift, which empowers a man to believe,
Is marvellous and simple, like a gift of light. . . .
Not to the sightless, but to men with eyes, who wander
    groping in the night.

(*pause*)

"This wine is corked, Ricardo," Anselmo said.
Ricardo took the glass, and smelled it. "Well, that's that,"
He sighed, and rang for Metcalf. "Metcalf's gone to bed,
I think," said John. "Well, let him get up. Metcalf lies flat
On his back twelve hours out of the twenty-four.
And he's exceptionally well-paid. That's my last *Chateau
    Lafite*, Anselmo, and a fine

Year, 1920; it's sad; I had saved the bottle for you.
Would you like another *Médoc*, or a somewhat heavier
    wine?—
I've a *Clos de Vougeot* '23; and I've a few
Vosne-Romanée, but it's '24, not a good year
For Burgundy. Come down to the cellar. Be an hour before
                        Metcalf'll appear."

*   *   *

JOHN

The old and the young might live together in peace, even in
    this new day,
If there were room for all.
But the empire of Nippon is small;
The Germans are cramped; the Italians are over-crowded;
    elbow-room
Is what we fight for.

And do not forget, when the census of the pullulating
Masses is taken, the census of the prolific machines
Whose tally is not told.

How many men, plus how many machines, can flourish in a
    given area?

CARL

In a capitalistic state?—*huit chevaux—quarante hommes.*

RICARDO

Men fight for empire, not for elbow-room.
We fight because that's our breed, that blood is in us.

We're one part wire-hair, two parts German shepherd,
And the rest—the rest—oh, call it Corsican corporal
In a wee grey *redingote* and a blue-ribbon stance.

We're built in the image of the elder gods, the jealous,
Truculent, tricky, ignorant gods of Rome.
Jove we understand, a heavy drinker, an incorrigible
Addict of fancy-dress, a pouncer upon virgins;
And Juno, curling her lip at his senile capers,
And under her boredom hatching mischief for all;
And Venus, lifting her chin this way and that
Before her mirror, or opening her blue eyes wide
In an innocent stare, while her nipples pucker and harden.
And Mars we understand.
                                    But Jesus not.
Charity is an uneasy graft on the tree of Man.
Charity is a sport; it is paler and has an extra petal;
It is not characteristic of the species; it is not *echt* Man.

ANSELMO

And three-parts beast—is that *echt* Man, Ricardo?

Why should you take it for granted, because we live here
        and now, not there and formerly,
That we are resolved, that we are concluded, that no further
        fermentation, let us say, is possible,
That there is nothing now for us to do
But to age, to mellow in our type?

This unrest, these wars,
Is not that still perhaps the boiling of the must—red grapes
        so lately green?

And may not Charity perhaps be Man's essential savour,
The rare bouquet of a princely vintage: MAN?

CARL

It may indeed!—But Man, in his capitalistic wars,
Ferments as soup ferments, gone sour in the pot. No future
To that!
Only in revolution, only in the audible seething of the crushed
    masses
Does Man ferment to a purpose, to his proper destiny. Wine
Such as Hebe never poured for bibbling Jove, may come of
    this;
But it will come of nothing else.

As for Charity, we've had enough of Charity—even the kind
    you mean—
And anyway, Charity is a dirty word, it's gone to bed
Too often with philanthropists, it's *effututa*.

*   *   *

RICARDO

It does not matter. Two wars in a generation must so debase
Those whom it does not destroy, that to remain alive,
For the bespattered remnant of the unhappy human race
Will hardly, in any important way, be to survive.
Science will remain alert, surgery
Will cut away the poisoned leg, men will find
That they can get about on crutches, and still in some way be
Themselves, though lopped;
But how shall the bleeding in the will-to-live be stopped?
What shall we do for gangrene in the mind?

No man will come unscathed
Out of this brothel; in a clean shirt and freshly bathed
We shall drink coffee with cream, peruse
In a shackled paper the manacled news
(Some of us will, that is, those of us who remain)
But the shell that does not blow the head
Into unsuspected fragments, makes none the less its furrow
    in the brain.
We shall have lost our innocence . . . of which it might be said
That it is not like hair, which renews
Itself, but like a tooth which once extracted does not grow
    again.

A man may go to war—go to his first war, that is, out of con-
    fusion; but to go to war twice
Indicates either callousness, or vice.

JOHN

During the years of my own innocence, that is to say before
The steamy cooking in the pot of this snakes'-brew,
This second war,
I believed in man, in his essential goodness; I *knew*
No nation would attack the undefended, the disarmed,—
But now, having been defiled, I do not trust
So far.
All helpless things are harmed,
Humiliated, driven into a littered corner, raped, shot running
By the Beast enthroned. . . . I had not thought of that. . . .
Man being not man as I had hoped, but utter beast
Tramples out the argument; we *must*
Build fences against the marauding forest . . . at least
If we care to continue under so sad a condition, in so sick a
    disgust.

Well, don't ask me, of course; you're probably right;
I'm out of my depth with all you high-brows; but,
One thing I do know: there's lots of men that love a fight;
And war—don't you see—it takes them out of their rut.
No responsibility, either; nothing to do
But get up with the bugle and go where you're damned well
    told;
Like being a child . . . trying to get away with things, too.
Well, you may get killed, of course, but you don't get old.
I know what you mean, I get you all right, but—well—
It's good for a man now and then to get away from his wife,
No matter how much he may love her; and anyway, hell!—
I never had such a good time in my life!
You say we're in for another: it looks to me not.
But if we did get into another, I'd go like a shot.

JOHN

You are the salt of the earth, Pygmalion,—and the end of
    the world.
You are my enemy till we all lie quiet and the gas-cloud
    clears.
How long will that be?—Surely in a dozen years
We should be the best of friends.
        You are not loud for empire—yet the flag of peace
    is furled
And wrapped about its standard in the wind of your talk;
    and effort shrivels and is curled
Like a sensitive-plant for hours after you have touched it;
    pall-borne by its peers
At your suggestion a civilization in arrears
To destiny, pays up, trots graveward, and the squealing pipes
    are skirled.

You are my enemy to the end of time, which is not far,
I think, as things look now . . . and the salt of the earth;
You sweeten on the tongue the tainted every-day
Of stodgy striving; but I see you as you are:
A man who would provoke disaster, in adventure's dearth;
And I laugh out of a bandaged mouth at what you say.

RICARDO

War is man's god; he has but one.
And Peace, but the time it takes the unhorsed warriors to
    mount and come on.

ANSELMO

There is no peace on earth today save the peace in the heart
At home with God. From that sure habitation
The heart looks forth upon the sorrows of the savage world
And pities them, and ministers to them; but is not implicated.
All else has failed, as it must always fail.
No man can be at peace with his neighbour who is not at
    peace
With himself; the troubled mind is a trouble maker.

There is no freedom like the freedom of a man who sees his
    duty plain
And does it without demur; the edges of the torn brain
In him knit properly and heal;
The jangled bells are tuned, and peal
Once more from the sunny belfry in a morning clear and mild
Like to those mornings when he woke and wondered
What rapture was in store,—and it was only the simple day!
Bright mornings when he was a child.

How sweet when the battle is lost to unbuckle from the weary
    shoulders
The straps that cut and gall,
And let the heavy armour fall;
Let clatter to the floor and abandon where it lies
The shield whereon he took
All day shock upon shock
Of the opposing lance, his angel in disguise.

The act of complete submission to the Divine Will
Is to you an ignominious act,
An expedient of the cruelly pressed, an ugly pact
To save the soul at the expense of the soul's pride:
A mess of pottage in exchange for a princely heritage denied.
Can you not see that to surrender darkness to light is to be
    still
Valiant, and more valiant than before, and at length victor?
Or do you think so ill
Of light, as such, that it must walk in your Triumph as
    planned, and the way for it cleared
By a blind lictor?

*   *   *

Anselmo said, and took in his brown hands
Quietly the small ebony crucifix
That hung between his knees, "Knowledge expands,
And men grow canny; yet if they cannot mix
Science and Jesus, they leave Jesus out—
Though Science, like the ogre on the mat,
Turns into fog, snake, demon, leaves in doubt
His face for ever; and Christ has not done that.

Out of such peace as can be troubled only
By your distress, I spoke; and I have erred.
You heard me through with deference; I saw plainly
You strove to get my drift—and got no word.
I am chagrined, like one who has defined
The colours of sunset to a friend born blind."

After a solemn pause, Anselmo said,
"I think I'll play some Bach, if you can stand
My noise. Go right on talking, please"; and spread
Over the pedals of the concert grand
Ricardo could not play, but kept in tune
Always, in hope someone might call who could,
His broad black boots, twitched up his gown, and soon
Built Peace—from felt, wire, ivory, and wood.

Nobody talked, although it seemed that some
Preferred to talk, were cowed into this hush;
Ricardo not—he cared not whence might come
This beauty, so it came; the mutinous flush
Of John said, Jesus had a champion there
Unjustly come by, tricky, not quite fair.

Anselmo closed the piano. "I'm afraid I must go,
Ricardo," he said; "I have some work to do.
Good-night to you all."
Ricardo went with him into the hall.
At the door Anselmo turned and said gently, in his fine voice
    free from unction and warm,

"*Dominus vobiscum;*" then looked at Ricardo with a look
   both quizzical and sad.
Ricardo, returning the look with deep affection, gravely replied,
"*Et cum spiritu tuo.*"

                         When they had left the room
Merton said, "Awfully nice fellow, Anselmo, I think."
"Swell guy," said Pygmalion.
John said, "Don't you think we all ought to go home?"
"Hell, no," said Pygmalion. "Where's my drink?"

Ricardo said, "Whatever the case for God, the splendour of
   Man
Can not be questioned.
This Music, this proud edifice erected
Out of reach of the tide
By drowning hands,
This deathless, this impeccable, projected
By peccant men, who even as they laboured sank and died,
Irrefutable witness to that splendour stands.

It speaks more loud
Than the waves that batter
The wild bluff:
There is no God.
But it does not matter.
Man is enough."

42

"He plays very well," said Merton.
                              "Why weren't you listening,
Then?" said Carl.
                    John said, "Ricardo,
You don't know everything."

PYGMALION

I'm one of those people that Stravinsky just can't stand:
I listen to music with my eyes shut; there I sit,
With my languorous eyelids shielded by my long white
    hand. . . .
And if you think I'm posing, or at prayer, or have just been
    hit
By the cocktails I had before dinner, why, have it your own
    way.
I find I can listen more intently when I don't have to look
At the coat-tails of Narcissus, or wonder if anybody's going
    to play
The harp, or how much saliva came out of the horn the fellow
    shook.

Musicians, of course, always watch the performers or follow
    the score;
And it makes you sort of wistful when you realize how much
    they must know.
Yet I can't help wondering if, really, they wouldn't get more
Out of the music, just as music, with their eyes closed, even so.

A man may be a musical genius or just a music-loving
  dunce,—
But he can't give his undivided attention to two things at
  once.

RICARDO

I find no flaw in your logic, yet apparently he can.
It would seem that to watch the musicians not only does not
  hinder, but enhances,
Completes the music for the professional musical man.

PYGMALION

But is that because he's interested in the music, or because it
  advances
His ego in some way?
     I find that when I come up for air out
  of those trances
Which are actually a more concentrated listening than my
  mental pocket can afford,
And look around at the musicians in the audience it always
  seems to me that the moment they're not jealous, they're
  bored.

JOHN

An artist is bound to be jealous when he considers that the
  public's being fooled
By a showy second-rater, especially if he himself has sort of
  been left out in the rain;
But let something really fine come along, all jealousies are
  pooled
In a common admiration; I've seen it happen time and again.

LUCAS

How can Stravinsky know how Pygmalion feels about music,
  any more than Pygmalion knows how Stravinsky feels?

44

Personally, I never could get excited about musicians; I don't
    think they're genuine; I think they're a lot of rhinestone
    heels.

PYGMALION

In any case, they shouldn't write books; they shouldn't even
    open their mouths except to tell
Marvellous malicious stories on each other; at that they're
    swell.

PART II

"I want to talk," said Lucas, "about love!"
And gripped his hands until his knuckles gleamed.
He spoke in a loud voice, then did not move
Or make a sound for a long time, it seemed.
Then suddenly he surged forward in his chair:
"I want to ask you what it is you do
When someone, that you had, just isn't there,
And never will be, when you know it's through.

I know, of course, that you forget in time
And feel the same as if you hadn't been
Ever in love, or almost so; but I'm
Asking you, what do you do all in between?
Of course, I've got my job, and all of that,"
Said Lucas; "that's not what I'm getting at."

"This girl," said Lucas—"none of you know her name,
So I can say this—she was engaged, you see,
To another man when I first met her; she came
To visit my sisters, and she played around with me
Of course, quite a lot; I was crazy about her right from the
  start,
But I wouldn't let myself go, because I knew
About this man, and I didn't want to get hurt
If I could help it. Well, that all fell through.

One day she kissed me. And then, well, after that day
We were hardly apart for a minute, I couldn't bear her out of
  my sight;
I was sure she meant to marry me—though she never did
  say
She would, I remember now—well, the other night
She called me up: her family had made a fuss, she said,
And she was marrying this chap. I said, 'O.K., go ahead.'"

"Women are poison, and I prefer my poison straight.
This two-or-three drops at breakfast in your orange-juice,
Five-or-six drops, say seven, better make it eight,
In your after-dinner coffee,—that's abuse
Of the system, and abuse of the drug, whose ill effects,"
Pygmalion said, "are due to the under-dose
Over-administered. The man who gets married expects
To sip up heaven; and in a year he's comatose:

Can't stand her, can't get along without her, kicks,
Curses, flatters, fawns,—oh, drink 'em by the cup,

I say! and none of their niggling, shifty tricks . . .
You're either in paradise or you throw 'em up!
All right, go marry one," Pygmalion said;
"And have her found in your stomach after you're dead!"

"Yes, there's a long list of items to that bill by the time you
    come to foot it,
Me lad," Pygmalion continued. "As Ogden Nash might put
    it:
They're always wanting attention, and if you don't feel like
    kissing them every minute of the day it's a misde-
    meanour;
And right in the middle of the season they send your shoot-
    ing-clothes to the cleanour."

MERTON

And when you've got a fellow in for a drink and want to
    have a talk with him they keep watching him to see
    where he sets his glass down.

PYGMALION

And they fill the place so full of Early American furniture
    that there isn't a comfortable chair in the house where
    you can set your ass down.

MERTON

And when you get your bath-towel pretty wet wiping your
    hair
They put it back in the bath-room with a patient smile and
    show you the mark it made on the back of the chair.

LUCAS

And when you have company if you don't act as if you had
    finger-bowls every day they're simply furious.

47

Pygmalion

And every four weeks or so they're likely to burst into tears
and behave very curious.

Merton

And they use your last razor-blade and get it all dull and
don't tell you a word about it.

Lucas

And when you ask them what they did with your old white
sweater you can tell by their guilty look they've given
it to the Good Will but they pretend they've never
heard about it.

Pygmalion

And they're always saying, "Now don't interrupt me!" and
always interrupting, and they can't let anything drop.

And they insist on telling long stories, which they do very
badly, because they never know what to leave out or
where to stop.

Merton

And they think they have an acute sense of humour, and if
they make a *gaffe*,

And catch you grinning, they say, "That wasn't what I
meant, and you *know* it! What I *meant* was—no, *listen!*
—Oh, all right, *laugh!*"

Pygmalion

And they're either afraid you're about to say something im-
proper and making you hush,

Or they're being a good fellow and telling dirty stories to the
wrong people and making you blush.

Merton

And when you've caught an awful cold in your head and feel
sick as a cat

Instead of saying they're sorry they say, "Now I wonder
how you got that."

PYGMALION

And they leave lip-stick on cigarette-butts and napkins and
all around your mouth and on your collar.

MERTON

And when they buy something for 2.98 instead of 3 they
think they've saved a dollar.

LUCAS

They believe in the equality of the sexes and in equal wages
for women and men.
And then they invite you out to have a cocktail with them
and do they pay for it? Guess again.

MERTON

And if you think they look nice and say, "Is that a new
dress?" they exchange glances with some other woman.

PYGMALION

And they pride themselves on having a masculine mind when
as a matter of fact they're hardly human.

RICARDO

The family circumstance
Is man's by choice,
Woman's by function; hence
The acrid voice,

The pretty mouth down-curled
In bitterness,—
For whom the perilous world
Showed more than this.

The children borne and reared
Are underfoot,
To her who twice has heard
The homing brute

Enter the hall, and shake
Away the weather,
And man and arm-chair make
A sigh together.

The snorting wind that paws
The decorous door
Speaks in a language hers,
Though heretofore

Hushed, like a healthy rogue
Who would avow
Their common childhood's brogue
To the lisping Now.

Save for her slippered spouse
That fireside
To the wind and the wind's news
Would be opened wide.

But here he sprawls unspurred,
And must be rested . . .
From dangers not incurred
Till weighed and tested.

MERTON

(*to Pygmalion*)

And now he's going to marry her, the damned fool. *Pretty
    little filly,*
But just a cheap plater. You know the strain.

PYGMALION

                                        Know it well:
"White Breasts" out of "Black Velvet" by "Midnight."
But if he's happy, what the hell?

* * *

PYGMALION

I can't make love to a woman I really respect.
It's an awfully personal thing, no matter what you say;
It's a thing you can't share; and a woman you love, or respect,
Why, she might be thinking, or something, and it gets in your
    way.
Kind I always fall for, too, and that's the odd
Thing about it; I *like* 'em brainy and aristocratic;
But for—well—I want somebody who thinks I'm just about
    God,
Or whose attitude toward me is more or less automatic.

I've thought sometimes I'd marry; I'd like to have a son,
I don't know why, I'd just like to have a kid,—
Two, maybe, even three, but anyway one—
But a woman wouldn't stand for me, be a fool if she did;
And it wouldn't be fair to her, either, if our embarrassed re-
    lation
Were as rare as the elephant's, and solely for procreation.

51

"Lucas, Romantic Love is on the rocks,
Battered to kindling, flotsam on every shore,
Her sails as furled as are the *Antioch's*
Square sails," said Merton; "she will sail no more.
A gallant ship; but shipping in our day
Can't trust to winds to puff it where 'tis bid;
We can't go on rounding the Cape that way—
Where'd progress be, and coffee, if we did?

No man can tell what treasure in the teak
Of that exotic hold, a Spaniard's prize,
Went bubbling down, was questioned for a week
By dense myopic fish with lampy eyes;
Thank heaven, though, the old oil-burner's there
When I've a deal on and no time to spare."

"That's not the point," Carl said, "the point is not
Whether you get your contract or get the air;
We're about as through with this thing called Love as—
          what?—
Plumes in our helmets, powder on our hair.
Love's lazy, won't keep step, is all the time
Swooning into a dozen lilies, or under a yew,
Or looking backward, and bursting into tears and rhyme;
Holds everything up, just can't fit in, won't do.

I've died for love myself—oh, yes, I have,
Don't worry—but after what I've read and seen
I've got to be in the current; I'd sooner not live
Than be a spumy stick in a back-wash, if you see what I
    mean.
And the man who travels by the *Bremen* and lies on her deck
Longing for the old square-rigger gives me a pain in the
    neck."

"It's true, the lilies are beginning to fester a bit,"
Ricardo said; "who wrote that awful line?"
"Why . . . it was Andrew Marvell, wasn't it?"
Said Merton doubtfully. "Your guess is as good as mine,"
Threw in Pygmalion. "Drayton," ventured John.
"*I* wouldn't know," said Lucas. "Percy Bysshe
Shelley's my guess," said Carl; "but what about it? Get on
With it! You were saying—" "Doesn't sound very Shelleyish
To me," said Merton, "let alone Shelleyan . . . oh, well,
It'll come to me later." "I was about to say: it seems
Even to my nostrils that the lilies are beginning to smell;
And that the time has come to deck our amorous themes
With the honester stenches—tansy, feverfew . . ."
"Why, Dick!" said Carl; "you little idol-breaker, you!"

"I know something about *you*, Carl, I could tell,
If I wanted to," said Pygmalion. "Why leave Lucas all alone
    like this? You know damn well
Why you're back from Russia two months early,—and so
    do I!

You had dinner with the charming reason Wednesday night.
I saw you at the *Lafayette*. Oh, my, oh, my!
You had plumes in *your* helmet, all right!"

Carl blushed a little, and said, "God, are you *everywhere*?"
"'*Art Thou*,' is the proper usage," said Pygmalion. "The
lay brother will now lead us in prayer."

* * *

RICARDO
(to Carl)

If you lived in the north, you would know what words over-
    winter
Untended in that climate: *peony—phlox—*
Never, in the north, would you leave untended for the winter
Camellia, holly, box.

Love is a word indigenous to every soil,
Herbaceous but perennial; unscrupulous Nature
Has need of it; starve it, hack it,—it will recoil
To its root . . . and rise anew to its ancient stature.

Comradeship, today however stout,
Is a word that man must feed
Daily, and plant from seed
Each year, or it dies out.

MERTON
(to John)

It is difficult for you to believe that the surgeon, when he cuts
    you open, does so primarily

Not to save your life, or even in the interest of science, but
    because he wants
A new Purdy gun.

It is difficult for you to believe that the preacher who so
    earnestly exhorts you, does so primarily
Not to save your soul, or even in the interest of the Church,
    but because his daughter
Wants a badminton set, one of the expensive kind.

We go too far in our insistence upon heroism among humble
    men—to what extent heroic
Are our own activities?
It is romantic to assume that because a man buttons his col-
    lar behind
He cannot be in debt to his laundress.

The surgeon cuts you open because he needs a thousand dol-
    lars, or, if he has a thousand dollars,
Because he must keep up his skill, just as a pianist must,
By playing scales, by daily making incisions
In abdomens painted yellow with picric acid.

The last thing he thinks about is you.

It is in the interest of the husband and father whose profes-
    sion is
The expounding of the Word,
To excite, to seduce, by no means to repel or estrange
His congregation.

How could it be otherwise? We ask too much. Heroism

Is rarer than the unicorn. By report, it is not extinct.
But for a man with a family, heroism is out of the question.

JOHN

Heroism is out of the question, if you like, except for heroes.
    But there have been
And without a doubt still are heroic men
In both professions,—not all of them bachelors, either.
Heroism is a private pact between a man and his destiny.
His wife and children are out of it. But men like myself and
    you
Will continue to excuse our lack of courage in a crucial mo-
    ment by saying, as in your case, "You see,
It's impossible. I'd do it; only I have to consider my family";
Or as in my case, "I can't. I haven't the guts. But, God,
    what the right woman could have made of me!"

*   *   *

(*Pygmalion overhears a remark of Merton to John*)

"Why, you never were alone in your life! You couldn't stand
    it
To be alone for a minute!" said Pygmalion. "You'd howl
    your head off till you heard
Footsteps in the passage—Nurse coming with a light! Oh,
    I'll hand it
To you, you're fond of reading—books about Solitude pre-
    ferred;
But you like to read them with your door wide open, and
    guest after guest

Grinning in with a glass in his hand and saying, 'How 'bout it,
Old Bookworm? What about being sociable and joining the
    rest
Of the boys in a little poison?'—well, did you ever close that
    door? I doubt it."

Merton was angry. He flushed, and a pretty mean look
Came into his eyes. He was a man who loved a story on him-
    self, would worm it
Out of you, and laugh the gayest of all, but he'd brook
No levity on the subject of his being a lone-wolf and a her-
    mit.
Two other convictions he had, you mightn't take a crack at,
    which
Were The Menace of the Jews, and The Over-Taxation of
    the Rich.

*   *   *

MERTON
(to John)

You're mad! You're raving mad! (Forgive me if I seem a bit
    abrupt)
But the Supreme Court is the *only* institution we have that
    is *not* corrupt!

JOHN

Not corrupt? Is it only money that corrupts? Mortality
Corrupts! How often
Do you meet a man of eighty with his faculties unimpaired?
    —with his memory exact?—No matter how honourable,
    no matter how wise
He is at sixty, your Judge who has a job for life, his arteries
    will harden and his brain will soften,

And he'll be interpreting justice for the living while he's
    dying,—if he does it until he dies!
It's as ridiculous to have a man of eighty as to have a boy of
    eighteen
Interpreting the Constitution; what we need is the man in
    between.

MERTON

That depends on the man! If the man is the henchman of an
    irresponsible despot
We do not need him! Of what use to the country will be
The healthy faculties of a man in his prime if those faculties
    are employed
To trick us, to bleed us, to put the screws on what's left of
    our independence?—Will he,
Supposing his mind *is* more agile than the mind of an elderly
    man, use that agility
To our advantage?—Don't tell me
That a fine intelligence even at the age of eighty, combined
    with a scrupulous integrity—
Oh, don't be a fool!

JOHN

As long as you say, "Don't *be*,"
All right; but if you call me a fool again, I'll punch your nose.

MERTON

And that, even though I *am* senile and doddering and leaning
    on a stick, I suppose!

PYGMALION

Oh, for Christ's sake, can't you let the poor benighted
    bitched-up country go to hell in peace, and quit yapping
    about it?

*Democratic—Republican—*to hear you fellows talk you'd
    think there was
Some essential, some organic difference between the two,
As between female and male!
Why, I tell you there's not a candidate for office in either
    party who wouldn't turn
Hermaphrodite in a minute if he thought it would get him
    a vote!

No, the world's got out of hand while we've been busy
Winging grouse and driving into bunkers and dodging our
    income tax.
Democrat or Republican at the bedside, the patient will die.
Give the poor old girl two minutes of silence, say I.

*   *   *

Merton
(to Carl)

It's not so much that it's bad art; after all, there's plenty
    of good art;
But it's bad propaganda.
Whom do you convince but the people already in line with
    you?—A fine
Recruiting-sergeant you'd make!

You scorn to write like a poet; that pen's too warm still
From the hand of the bourgeoisie.
No, no, you've got to write like a turbine, like a riveting-
    machine, like an electric-chair;
And if people can't understand you, why, that's their affair.

The trouble with you communists is, you're the biggest
    snobs on earth, and the greatest
Egotists.
You'd go through the fire for your party;
But your party could die of dry-rot before you'd insert so
    much as a comma into your verses
To elucidate your party's splendid vision to a puzzled
Earnest millionaire.

RICARDO

Proletarian poetry today is the private scream
Of the individual encroached upon by the mass.
It is the love-song of the claustrophobiac who has espoused
    the crowd.

Walled in by the flanks of the herd,
The egregious spirit against its given word and against its
    will withdraws
To its only breathing-place, to the small open centre;
Whence with most passionate fisty hand
It urges-on the herd in a voice they trust but in a language
They do not understand,
And from a shrinking circle variably approaching nothing-
    ness, which none the less they shall not enter.

Safe on its diminishing island sits the surrounded *I*. . . .
And loves to this extent the tide it is diminished by:
"Thou rock, my soul, be stern against the eroding sea!
Thou strong, thou laminated thing!
Yield to the welcome, to the invited wave
All, all thy streakèd substance, save
The jewel at its core!
Eat me, ye hungry; but let food suffice—

One morsel more
Were ritual, were unseemly sacrifice."

Never were poets so "hidden in the light of thought."

CARL

And never were liberals so busy grinding axes
Between the upper and the nether mill-stones.

Thou shell!—thou Chambered Nautilus!

(to Merton)

You came into this world equipped. Fully-armed,
Like Minerva from the head of Jove, you sprang
From the brow of the fostering epoch,—and the morning
    stars all sang;
Equipped and unalarmed
Proceeded to live life, a god
Dispensing favours, shaking out thunders with a sharp nod.

We are MAN, emerging again out of the dark past; this is
    the second coming
Upon the earth of MAN.

This creature, unfamiliar even to himself, will stare at himself
In wonder, watch his wonderful hands, and say,
"Who are they?"—

Stare at the red star near the Pleiades,
The red star in Orion, and say,
"Who are these?"—

Say this with his wonder and with his pleasure,—with his
   mouth not yet.
This crude and beautiful being not only is beset
By inclement forces wailing above him, breeding underneath;
He is put to the task of hewing once again
Out of the primal throat with pain
WORDS . . . and of speaking them, with a tongue that only
   yesterday
Served but to roll his meat against his teeth.

"Shakespeare!" cried Merton.
            "Where?" said Pygmalion. "Are you sure?
What else do you see?"
            "No, no,—the line! The line!"

Pygmalion said, "There, there!
(Keeper, bring a rope and secure
This patient to his chair
While I gag him—did he bite your finger?—well, he bit
   mine.)"

"Idiot," said Merton, and laughed. "I mean it was Shake-
   speare that wrote that line.
I don't agree that it is an awful line; it reads:
'Lilies that fester smell far worse than weeds.'"

                    *   *   *

MERTON
(to Pygmalion)

Oh, well, I don't know; he'd spent the last thirty years
Providing for 'em, and I suppose it seemed the only way
To keep on providing: insured right up to his ears,
You know. I saw him only the other day,
Played golf with him. It never even entered my head
He was so hard up. He talked about the flower show—
Crazy about chrysanthemums; always went to see them, he
    said—
I said I hadn't been there yet but I intended to go.
Next thing I heard—no, carbon monoxide; found
Dead in his car in the garage; his daughter found him, Jill,
Sophomore at Wellesley.

PYGMALION

And I suppose they all drive around,
Buy bathing-suits, go to the movies, do the marketing, still
In the same old bus?

MERTON

Oh, no, they've turned it in, I'm told. . . .
But then, they would have anyway; it must have been six
    years old.

*   *   *

RICARDO

Some hours of death to this beleaguered mind would be of
    benefit.

Slumber no longer revives with its pure stream
The shrunken, folded flagon.

If death could be bought in tablets and administered at will,
    —O true apothecary!

The heart, whose only office is to beat, beats on, is not con-
    fused;
If yesterday it staggered, it does not remember.

The mind, however, slides on the loose heap of its piled in-
    adequacies. Degrading
That consciousness cannot even for a moment to its own ends
    enslave
This throned invertebrate, this loutish Death.

*   *   *

"Not that the world is so much with us," Merton
Remarked, "but such a world! It seems to me
It's getting noisier every day; I'm certain
'Tis more uncivil; men of low degree
In high positions—is there any hope
For culture, think you, when the grocer's son
Rides in his car, with judges and the Pope
To entertain him through the microphone?

Come, let us, like those gentlefolk of Florence
Who fled the pest in the Italian tale,
Absent us with some haste and much abhorrence
From these mephitic shores and, setting sail
For some green island, loll on delicate thrones
Till Doomsday, swapping yarns and skipping stones."

CARL

Yes, pack your bags—I beg your pardon, let
Your valet pack your bags, and get the hell
Out of here, do! Work up a little sweat
Shaving yourself some day, you'll feel just swell.
Meantime there's Florence; and in a nasty state,
What with more plagues than one, what with the poor
Cleaning the privies of the rich—relate
That jest in your Decameron, be sure.

You don't like things the way they are; you'd like
A change. A change is coming; and it's near.
But not a change you'll relish; at least you strike
Me so.—The trouble with all you people here
Is: two of you lie, two trifle, and the rest can't think.
Yes, I'll shut up. No, I don't want a drink.

"Your masses," Merton said, "yes, yes, I know
It's not their fault; they've not been treated well—
Whatever the cause may be, their tastes are low,
Their conversation tedious, and they smell.
I hope they get their heaven, achieve their goal,
Have a good time, be free—but where's the hurt
If I, while loving a man's immortal soul,
Deplore his manners and dislike his dirt?

Why should you hate my guts because my pants
Are pressed, my coat fits, and my nails are clean?
Is not the idea: *all* men should have the chance
To bathe, *et cet.*—or just what *do* you mean?
You don't add up. Or is it possible
You honour the dirt, and not the man at all?"

"It's true I honour the dirt; that's perfectly true,"
Carl answered, hastily lighting a cigarette,
And rising to his feet; "and so would you
If you'd seen such men as I have, with their sweat
Running like tears and making their chests all muddy,
Men second to none, I tell you!—well, it just looks queer
To me, clean finger-nails on a hand as bloody
As hell—that's why when I look at you I sneer.

Why does Anselmo honour that ugly thing
He wears around his neck?—I'll tell you why:
That's where the man he loves hung suffering
Till he can't tell the man from the cross. Well, neither can I.
I honour the dirt, if you like," Carl spoke from the door,
"Because it is the dress my mother wore."

Over the sound of flushing water, which,
For some strange reason, science having gone so far,
Even in the houses of the extremely rich
Still roars in a room, and everybody knows where you are,
Pygmalion said, "Well, Merton, what do you think?
Has Swatter any chance?" "Race didn't fill,"

66

Merton replied. "Say, can I have a drink
For God's sake?—no, mine's Bourbon.—It's just as well;

A mile's too short for him. Cloud Sweeper's running."
    "Who's up?"
"Bobby Jones." "Any odds?" "Ought to be." "Do any hurt
To put a little something on her nose?" "Well, this is no
    tip;
You do what you like. I'm going to bet my shirt."
Carl came back. "Who did the etching on the right?"
Somebody said, "Benson." Carl said, "Who's got a light?"

"You spoke rather as a poet, did you not?—and an in-
    dividual,
Just now, than as a member of your party?" Merton said to
    Carl: "surely
The orthodox approach to Marxism is not an emotional one."

                                        "Any approach,"
Carl answered, "to the Truth, is an orthodox approach. It
    is a proper question though.
I spoke for myself, of course. But it would be useless to deny
That most any man who in his boyhood saw his mother die
Too young, of no disease but poverty, and recalls how he was
    unable either to earn or beg
Even so much as a warm coat for her, will turn a yellow eye
On the ermine wraps getting out of the motor-cars and going
    into the theatres, and they will look to him like snow
Where a dog has lifted his leg.

Adult allegiance to an intellectually-conceived inevitable
proletarian dictatorship, does not exact,
Necessarily, repudiation of a childhood memory, a humiliat-
ing and meagre
Personal experience, which as a matter of recorded fact
Was largely instrumental in bringing about that stumbling
"approach" through a pitch-dark wood
To the light of a camp-fire, and friendly faces ruddy in that
light, and eyes courageous and eager,
And intellectual companionship, and a plan, and all things
good.

PYGMALION

Companionship, and eagerness, and presumably a modicum
of courage and possibly a plan,
I concede you,—but *Intellect*?—in this friendly, seated-about-
the-fire man?

To you, as to all enamoured, the face of the beloved is fault-
less;
You have not seen him frenzied from sacramental wine and
spitting Billingsgate
Upon the observer; you do not hear him
Babbling violence, weightless, meaningless and saltless;
What you hear is a partisan roar, and that is all, you are so
near him.

You're all for the workers of the world getting together and
making it snappy, and it does you credit,—
But listen, buddy, did you ever happen to read any of those
newspapers you edit?

"Look here," said Carl to Merton, "let's get this straight:
You've your own personal approach to things, and so have I;
You sit there thinking—well, what are you thinking?—that
    it looks as if you've got the second filly
To win the Kentucky Derby; or about a new dry fly
That's named after you; I'm sitting here thinking—well,
    what?—that I don't much like, say,
Suede shoes on men, or about an article I'm writing on
    Trotsky and Zinovieff,
Or maybe just sitting and drinking and thinking of a dog I
    had named Buster, and wanting to cry.

It doesn't matter what we're thinking; we don't have to think
    at all; we don't even have to act;
The dictatorship of the proletariat, though not yet present
    and in this room, is a fact!
It's present in its causes, like a bomb, that has just been
    dropped
From an air-plane, and hasn't hit the ground yet, but can't
    be stopped.
It's present in your class and in mine, in the struggle between
    them; it is the ineluctable economic effect
Of that struggle; in embryo still, if you like, yet if you had
    your ear to the ground
I think you would detect
A strange and rapidly approaching subterranean rumble,
    such as warns a man,
But never in time, of a major seismographic disturbance.
    Can you hear it? I think you can:
A somewhat hair-raising sound."

Pygmalion

Carl, my lad, do you ever stop to think
What a bore you are?——

Carl

I don't have to stop, to think.

Pygmalion

Very good. But don't you ever think to stop?
No sooner are you the bride of Socialism——

John

Oh, let it drop!

Pygmalion

No sooner are you penetrated by Socialism, than you begin
   to bulge
With Revolution; and from that moment on you indulge
Your interesting condition, by boring the world with raptur-
   ous slop
About the forthcoming Blessed Event!

Ricardo

Quite right. Or rather,
You've diagnosed the pregnancy; but you're wrong as to
who's the father.

Carl

Merton's the father. And he's just been told. And he's wild.

Ricardo

Merton's all for abortion; but the proletariat wants the child.

*   *   *

CARL
(to Merton)

Yet these yards and yards of the Brocaded Past, the longer
That cloak extends behind, the heavier is its drag upon the
    shoulders, and the shoulders no stronger
Than formerly. The time has come when we must choose:
Trailing this splendour we are trussed; we bear
Our shield without adroitness; and we wear
An encumbered sword, we cannot whip forth to use.

MERTON

A handsome metaphor. But I've grown shy
Of poetry. All these pictures for the eye,
Cadences for the ear—and in between,
Truth, crushed to earth and taking it, turning green.

RICARDO
(to John)

Babel is here, and now. Who speaks my language?—no one.
Science is so tall that no man sees its face:
This tower will not touch God.

The trick is this,—and it is a good trick, worthy a divine
Chicanery: in our impious determination
To build this bean-stalk, Science; climb it; peep
At Heaven through a key-hole; eaves-drop
On the ultimate Mystery; spy on God; learn all;
We have given eyes to one, and hands to another:
No man can both climb, and see.

We have specialized ourselves out of any possible
Acquaintance with the whole.

What man can build a motor-car? I build,
With the help of many hands and many brains,
One part, let us say, of the foot-rest of the accelerator. You
Work in the assembling-department; you bolt bolts
On things, all day.
What have you and I to say
To each other, about our work, or about a machine
We have never seen?

One man looks through a telescope at the spiral
Nebula in Andromeda; one
Photographs during eclipses the corona of the sun;
One sits in his study, calculates, computes,
Scribbles equations; refutes
A system of geometry.
Twelve men in all the world, let us concede,
Can read
His formulae.

The nearer the stars our battlements approach,
Reared by the stern and dogged wish
Of man to Learn—
The more we all talk gibberish.

Babel will not encroach
On Heaven, save at the cost
Of all communication lost. . . .

Wild mouths imploring desperate ears;
Wild eyes among the rainy Hyades,
Streaming with tears.

PART III

MERTON
(to Carl)

It is not at all necessary to call a spade a spade; it is only
    more dignified
To do so . . . a spade is a spade no matter what you call it.

Now that the house of Hanover is the house of Windsor, does
    the less German blood
Flow in the veins of Edward?
The *Avenue du Bois de Boulogne* has been re-named
The *Avenue Foch*;
The *Prado* is now the *Paseo de Marti*;
The name of the *Piazza di Spagna* is about to be changed,
I hear, to the *Piazza Generale di Bono*.
To what purpose? Why? What has been effected, beyond a
    wholesale
Re-painting of signs, and an inking-out of defunct addresses
On letter-heads?
                And will it be today,
When *St. Petersburg* is *Leningrad*, or tomorrow, when *Lenin-
    grad*
Is *Stalingrad*,
That a boatman on the Neva at night will ferry to the bay
In a weighted chest and drop over-board, out of sight
And out of fact the bones of the brilliant, gay
And cruel capital?
                When *Rome*

Is *Mussolinium,*
Will the Fountain of Trevi give me back my pennies? Will
the past be annulled?

Unfilial and boorish times: our splendid heritage
In pawn-shop windows!
Shall you not one day regret having given the royal dolls to
the children of the poor?—These, too,
Were your history. Only the past made possible
This outraged present.

Sack the palace if you must; if you need the *Gobelins*
For bed-quilts, take them.
But restrain, I beg you, if you have the time, the sticky
fingers
Of the children from smearing them.

CARL
(to Merton)

You want things just as they were when you first knew them;
you want nothing changed.
Things change, however, and the changing of their names is
also
Part of their history.
How far into the past shall we go back to please you?—to
the time when
The *Avenue du Bois de Boulogne* was called the *Avenue
De l'Impératrice?*
Would you like, perhaps, to see the fountains in the *Place de
la Concorde*
Playing in the *Place Louis Quinze?*
Shall the *Champs-Elysées* become again the *Nouveau Cours?*

74

And what will you call the *Avenue Victor Hugo*?—The *Avenue
     d'Eylau?*
The *Avenue de Saint-Cloud?*—would you like it by its original
     name, perhaps
The *Avenue Charles X?*
Would it please your wife, perhaps, to buy her Paris gowns
In a city named *Lutetia?*

No, no. You want things just as they were when *you*
First knew them—you want the Czar back; you want your
     youth back:
The carriages, the corsets, the cotillions, the favours and the
     fans.

All this means nothing to me; the English primrose pressed
     in your copy of Wordsworth
A pressed primrose is to me,
And it is nothing more. God, I'm so sick of the smell
Of faded personal tokens fluttering out from between the
     leaves
Of second-hand books!
                              Oh, let the dead past
Cremate its dead, I say! We have no room here even for
     its bones
In these city blocks that must house the living world!
                              MERTON
Something goes down with the ship even if all on board are
     saved:
You have left your jewels in the cabin.
                              CARL
We are rowing away from the suction of the sinking ship,
     and just in time.

If we have left our jewels in the cabin—it was either that
Or swirling about with them in the companionway, and the
    lights gone out.

We shall mine from the earth new gems, and set them in the
    nobler metals, do not doubt it.

But for the present we are busy trying to keep the oars in
    the rowlocks.

RICARDO
(to Carl)

Russia under Lenin is so many light-years away,
Its noble beam approaches you but now;
You stand transfigured in the golden light today
Of a star that, even while you bask in its bright ray,
Blackens, and disappears.
We must allow,
Perhaps, another nineteen years,
Before you see what's happening in Russia now.

CARL

Before you see it, with eyes turned so resolutely toward the
    west
We must allow another hundred years, at best. . . .
Except that long before then your shadow before you, black
    on the dazzling ground,
Will force you to look over your shoulder,—if not indeed to
    turn around.

MERTON
(to Pygmalion)

What?—did *you* ever fish that river?—*I* fished it one spring!
Never'll forget it—wild geese going over—weather grey, but
    the air

Soft as a feather—first time I ever heard a cuckoo, was there,
I remember well—funny my remembering—
The river at that point roared like Niagara, it was deafening.

That's where I took that salmon I started telling you about,
    the handsomest thing
I ever saw come out of the water, and the strongest,—
Though not the biggest—weighed just under thirty pounds.
He fought me till I thought it would get dark and I'd have
    to give up,—I didn't know which of us would live the
    longest;
Never saw such a determined cuss;—
If it hadn't been such hard work it would have been monot-
    onous.

He weakened finally, however, and I got him ashore.
Never saw such a beautiful salmon, either since or before.
Every colour of the sea, and every sunset colour.
Seemed a shame to kill it. I never felt so friendly toward
    anything in my life.
Why, in comparison to the way I loved that fish I never even
    liked my wife.
I called to Bill to come and see it, but of course he didn't
    hear.
And anyway, by the time he'd got there it would have faded
    and gone duller.
That was a wonderful year.

Funny my remembering that cuckoo. I remember, too,
Walking back through the wood,
The smell of the damp ground.
And the wind stirring in the leaves: I'd forgotten there
    could
Be such a gentle sound.

RICARDO
(to John)

The mind thrust out of doors,
And not a bone flung after
To hold between its paws
When night and hunger fall,
Leaves the warm house and all
Its grassy lakes of light,
And the good reek of supper;
And trots into the night.

The rabbits hear him come;
The wild-cat on the limb
Whittles its nails to knives,
And crouches over him.

Before the week is out
He leaps at the apple's throat
That hangs in the cold air;
Battens on bark and root,
That never ate such fare.

He harries the lean hill
In vain for winter vermin;
His blunted nose is still
To rabbit on the wind;
His coddled pads are softer
Than vixen's, and they bleed;
He stalks in bitter need,
With hope and belly thinned,
In vain the winter brook
For weasel turned to ermine.

When once the snow lies deep
He harvests where he can;
He wolfs the huddled sheep;
He drinks with drooling lip
The myriad stench of man.

MERTON
(to Pygmalion)

I don't know what ails him. Sound enough. I think he's
just plain lazy.

PYGMALION

That horse is sick, I tell you. Have you had the vet
Look him over?

MERTON

Not yet.

PYGMALION

You're crazy!
Valuable animal like that, and you neglect him as if he were
a human being!

MERTON

You think he's being tampered with?

PYGMALION

Well, it's possible, isn't it?—Anyway,
There's no harm in seeing.

MERTON

We claimed a horse today. . . .
"Night-shade" . . . out of a——

PYGMALION

I know the son-of-a-gun.

You'll have to run a rabbit in front of him, if you want *him*
    to run!

Full brother of that black mare, "Twinkler."
Bet my shirt on her at Bowie, including cuff-links, tie and pin.

MERTON

Where'd she come in?

PYGMALION

Come in?—Just ahead of the sprinkler.

RICARDO
(*to John*)

But how do you know, how do you really know you wouldn't
    enjoy
Eating from a fur spoon?—did you ever try it?
Precisely. Then how do you know?
Insist if you like that you don't like fur-lined gloves,
Fur caps, fur coats, fur collars,—I'll take you at your word.
But fur spoons,—how do you know?

Chestnuts, now, from a fur spoon might be charming.
Or grapes; wild rice, perhaps;
Possibly, too, that most delicious of all mushrooms, the
    marasmius
Oreades,—no, no,
How dull of me!—It is honey, surely, that should be eaten
From a fur spoon!

JOHN

Dick, you disgust me. You disgust us all.

RICARDO

                          Why so?
If I bring you some honey in a fur spoon, will you try it?

80

MERTON

(*to Pygmalion*)

Five hundred dollars,—and you couldn't clock a steam-boat
by it!

CARL

(*to Lucas*)

Taxation of all Church Property—that's the answer to that!

MERTON

(*to Pygmalion*)

Worked a mile in the mud the other morning in 1:40 flat.

CARL

In a State that has no State Church—and we deny that we
have—
The agnostic, to whom the Church is nothing, and the
atheist, who hates it, are forced to skimp and save
To pamper the Church—to make up a deficit that a taxed
Church Property would fill.
What a cheap and fraudulent life we live!—Take St. John
the Divine—
How much would I be taxed on that property, I wonder, if
that property were mine—
Believe me, plenty—and what of Trinity Church, and what
of Trinity Churchyard, standing there
Spread out over a whole square
Just where
Wall Street connects with Broadway,—
(Where the stem of Capitalism has its roots in the Church,
as one might say)
Untaxed!—How much would Merton have to fork out
In taxes every year, if that property belonged to him and
he conducted *his* business on it?

MERTON

About
Every penny I make, I shouldn't wonder. Still,
The Church does stand for something.

CARL

Stand for what?
Stands for getting something for nothing, and hanging on to
what it's got!
If property's to be taxed, in a State that has no State
Church, it should be taxed
Without benefit of clergy!
Too poor to pay taxes at home,
Are they?—They've plenty in the collection-plate, I notice,
to send a lot of nosey
Missionaries to China, and a lot of cosey
Fat dollars to Rome!

(*turning to Ricardo*)

Dick, did I hear you say that you prefer the Fairy-Ring
Mushroom to any other variety?

RICARDO

To almost any other thing!
Why?

CARL

Nothing. Only, so do I!
Where do you find them?

RICARDO

Mostly on the lawn, but in one of the pastures, too,
At Black Hall. I didn't know you knew
Anything about mushrooms!

CARL

Well, I do.
I know quite a bit about them, really; I think I know
At least forty edible varieties.

RICARDO

Is that so!
Could you come up to Black Hall
Some week-end early next fall?
We could have a lot of fun . . . I wish you would!

CARL

Thank you, I'd love to; I'm pretty sure I could.

RICARDO

Did you ever find a Caesarean amanita?

CARL

Yes, once.
Never was so excited in my life, but was I scared!
Dying to taste it, naturally, but afraid to take the chance;
Sent it to Washington to be identified, instead.
Beautiful thing—bright orange with a yellow stem
Standing in a white cup, and yellow gills—I really might
    have trusted *them*.
Report came back, "*Amanita caesarea*, excellent edible vari-
    ety. But beware
Of confusing this species with the deadly poisonous *amanita
    muscaria*"—which of course was why I'd sent it there.

MERTON

There were some things that looked like mushrooms growing
    on the golf-links,
Hundreds of them—look just like the real ones, the kind you
    buy,—and my wife thinks

They are. But I wouldn't let her touch them with a ten-foot
    pole—she doesn't know
The difference between mushrooms and toadstools any better
    than I do,
No matter how much she may insist.

RICARDO
(dreamily, catching Carl's eye)

"Mushrooms and toadstools."

CARL
(grinning)

Phrase invidious to the true mycologist.

MERTON

I found a puff-ball once that weighed four and three-quarter
    pounds.
I suppose that sounds
Like a whopper all right;
But I actually did; found it right by the road where we
    stopped for gas one night.
The man said we ought to cook it and eat it, said it was good;
So we said we would;
But of course we never intended to.

CARL

All puff-balls are edible so long as the flesh remains white.

RICARDO

As for myself, I must confess, I prefer them when they're
    beginning to be—well—
The colour of a gardenia you've worn all night in your lapel.

PYGMALION
(to Lucas)

Lot of restless old maids—nobody else to espouse, so they
    espouse a Cause!

Then it's back to Prohibition . . . and the rule of the Long-
Cotton-Drawers.

LUCAS

That's all very well; but the women aren't the only old maids:
Who's at the head of all these Anti-Vice Crusades?

RICARDO

(*overhearing*)

"Anti-Vice"—what a charming expression—a mind well-
stored
With such pleasant phrases, could never, I think, really be
bored.

(*to John*)

Since, however, the intelligible has failed us on every hand,
how shall we hope
For ransom save from the coffers of the unintelligible alone?
Only in madness, or in the meadows adjacent to madness, is
there scope
Today for the stride of the tall unshackled. What have we
known
That has not bound us? And shall we sit for ever bound,
Shuffling our chains into the yard for exercise at an appointed
hour, to keep the sick thing sound?

Too much has been explored; too great a tract of polar ice
Where not even God has walked since first he called it good,
is named "Marie."
Should we not insist upon the body's right to be drowned
In water unfathomed?—Why, no,—for there is no such sea.

85

The plummet has poked at our grave; the official lead
Knows all, there's not a word unsaid.

Who then would not depart with me
Into the Unpolluted, into the only Free?
Where Memory is a dissipating gas, where Reason
Draws off its boots; where to think twice
Is the only treason.

Let us go mad while there is yet time, under our own direc-
     tion, not wait
For the leisurely and outmoded spindle of an archaic Fate
To spin our destiny. Now, now, under the scrubbed skin
Jab neatly the unhygienic needle, thrust in
The fluid, drink
Like sand all proud excesses, all abandons, think
To the end of thought, and leave that rutted road
Abruptly where it ends, pursue
The faintly visible track
Until it widens and is smoothed out, and there is no road
     but you.

CARL

(to Merton, overhearing a remark of Merton to Pygmalion)

Widener offered a hundred thousand dollars for Brevity!
Big laugh.
Horse laugh.
Brevity laughed.
All the horses in all the barns laughed.
And all the horses' asses laughed.

"What could Widener *do* with a hundred thousand dollars?"

86

Come on, let's think for a minute and see if we can think of
    anything
That a man could do with a hundred thousand dollars if he
    had it to spare—a hundred thousand dollars
For the best answer.

*　*　*

MERTON
(to Carl)

Every man has a right to a job? *Right? Right?* What do you
    mean by *right*?
Every man has a right to roost in a tree, the right to propa-
    gate his species—
But supposing the forest-conservation-corps has cut all the
    trees down,
And the women all have died of lacquer-poisoning,
How does *Right* function then? Why, *Right* becomes then
As right as a trivet; and just as obsolete.

RICARDO

Be careful, Merton. You're talking good Karl Marx.

MERTON

Look at it this way, it's a matter of simple arithmetic:
We reduce the rate of infant mortality; we reduce the number
Of deaths by small-pox, typhus, yellow-fever;
We patch men up; we lengthen their lives; and at the same
    time
We increase the number of man-replacing machines.
What's going to happen? The Earth isn't getting any bigger;
And birth-control's taboo, except in the best families.
Of course, there's always war; but that seems a rather
Expensive way of answering the unemployment question.

87

CARL

The reason why there are three times as many men as there
    are jobs
Is because—and you know it as well as I do—one man is
    working the hours of three;
And the reason for that is that for a lot of smug and over-
    stuffed slobs
It's a hell of a sight more profitable that way, but it's a
    reason that doesn't appeal to me.
Now if you want to hear yourself make a fool of yourself go
    on and say
That suppose we do straighten it out, why, all that that
    means
Is a few years' respite, and then right back where we were
    . . . not with *you* out of the way
It doesn't, and the machines working for men, instead of
    men for the machines!

RICARDO

Let us grant that so long as the masses are imprisoned, and
    their common will to freedom declared,
Since the escape of each may depend upon the strength of
    all, all things with all are shared.
But why today in Moscow, with the masses in power, the
    thing accomplished, the majority enjoying its true will,
Is the dissenting mouth stopped up with unarguable lead, is
    Stalin still
Putting the opposition, which is perforce the minority, to
    death?

It is because, being no man's fool, he has no faith
Whatever in the continuing desire of the individual to stir
    into the common pot

88

That which (for so it has happened before and could again)
   might benefit him personally more tangibly if he did not.

It is because he dare not even for a moment forget that when
   the imprisoned men are freed,
Each walks into the open carrying his personal happiness,
   his vow to share all, and his greed.

MERTON
(to Carl)

That would explain why your permanent platform is com-
   posed
Exclusively of soft-wood planks:
By nailing ten poplars together you feel you have enclosed
A something *oaken* in the sill that must support successive
   ranks on ranks
Of arriving and evolving mortality; but when at last
Your imminent purpose is accomplished, the revolution past,
The wreckage washed along the gutters and the long bill paid,
Will people be content to live their broadening cultural lives
   upon a barricade?

CARL

No! Nor will there be any occasion for them to do so! There
   is a cultural life in Russia *today* which puts to shame
A thousand things which in this pretentious and self-satisfied
   country
Get by under that name.

I know what you mean by "culture": going to hear
The opera that was good enough for your grandfather, so it's
   good enough for you;

Shooing the women out of the dining-room after dinner; pre-
    ferring Bass's Ale to beer;
Buying the book, but reading it in the book-review;
Collecting glass, collecting Italian primitives, pretending
    you're spending
More than you can spare
For a variety of miscellaneous objects whose sole distinction
    is that they are either old or rare.

A thing might be beautiful as a dandelion-blossom—that
    won't do:
If it's *common* as a dandelion-blossom, right away, you're
    through.

Beautiful as a dandelion blossom, golden in the green grass,
This life can be.
Common as a dandelion-blossom, beautiful in the clean grass
Of the young, all-promising year;
Beautiful to the child: the eye of the child is clear.

Life itself is a weed by the roadside, a common, golden weed.
Give us back the eyes of our childhood, freed
From the squint of appraisal, the horny glint of greed!

Beautiful as a dandelion-blossom, golden in the green grass,
This life can be.
Common as a dandelion-blossom, beautiful in the clean grass,
    not beautiful
Because common, beautiful because beautiful;
Noble because common, because free.

*   *   *

MERTON
(to Carl)

You speak, my friend, in most ecstatic terms
Of life upon this negligible sphere;
An excellent protein, doubtless, for the worms,
Is Man,—but food for thought?—are you sincere?
It's true, at times a not inglorious figure
Leaps to a wave-crest and harangues the waves:
The Ship of State sails on, from fore to jigger
Her dirty decks aswarm with thieves and slaves.

I must confess, these recent altercations
Within the Left, between the Left and Right,
Have nipped somewhat my autumn aspirations
Toward Comradeship,—a budded thing, though slight.
Now, for your borshch of bullet-lead and jam
I would not give a tax-exempted damn.

RICARDO
(to Carl)

Having renounced Religion, that the State may stand un-
    fuddled,
Why come you marching hither in hordes, your faces wild
    and exalted?
What are these altars doing here in the Forum, and the reek
    of the warm, unsalted
Sacrifice,—the earth about the altars steaming and puddled?

There are men assembled in this place who have reports to
    consider, decisions to make; enter this Forum
With circumspection, please, and brush the leaves from your
    hair.

91

Listen, reflect, reject; if you have something to say, say it,
but with decorum.
Or drag your altars out into the jungle, and do your dancing
there.

PYGMALION

No use talking to him, Dick, it's too late, he's taken his
vows; the sluggard
Has definitely gone to the ant. The Marxian mind,
Repulsing the advances of Faith from the front, is buggered
By Faith from behind.

CARL
(*to Ricardo*)

And in return for my brushing the leaves from my hair, will
you,
Perhaps, Ricardo, remove the senatorial
Slightly brittle and brown large wreath of laurel
Which obscures somewhat your fine brow from the public
view?

Shall a man with a virulent and highly infectious disease
Be at large in the community? In what enlightened land
Is not pestilence checked, if possible traced to its source,
And there wiped out,—if possible, there wiped out?

And shall the workers of the Soviet republic, who are children still
(Though very bright children, I might add) in matters of
administration,
Be subjected to contact with the fetid effluvia of powerful
minds
All afflicted with what is to us the true Social Evil, not only
contagious but infectious?

In any modern society the dreaded germ is warred upon.
(As for me, you do not fear me: you have had one revolution,
   and you consider yourselves immune.)

*   *   *

RICARDO
(*in reply to a remark of Carl*)

Whether or not something was rotten in the state of Denmark
   in the fall of '32,
It is fascinating to watch our capitalist
United States go communist;
Touching to see Hearst and the bourgeois press commiserat-
   ing Trotzky, the way they do.

For what do they hope in return—World Revolution?—
   That could hardly be so.
No, no. Let Trotzky win the place
Of power that Stalin has, you'll see a far from slow
Right-about-face.

Capitalism is fostering the rift in the communist party,
That's all,—Trotzky is the wedge we drive
Into the rift, to split the rift wide.
In order to govern, we must first divide.

Part IV

Ricardo

In the Rotary Club and in the Communistic State there is
    no mourning
When Doctor Cog dies.
The place of Doctor Cog is immediately and automatically
    filled by Doctor Cog, and Doctor Cog and Doctor Cog
Are as alike as two cogs.

John said, "A man is tired of being a town all by himself.
He wants to be a grain of sand in a shovelful of sand in a
    cement-mixer
That is mixing cement to cement together the bricks in one
    of the walls
Of one of the buildings connected with one of the cement
    works
On the outskirts of a town."

Ricardo said, "Man has never been the same since God died.
He has taken it very hard. Why, you'd think it was only
    yesterday,
The way he takes it.

Not that he says much, but he laughs much louder than he
   used to,
And he can't bear to be left alone even for a minute, and he
   can't
Sit still.

You'd think he'd be glad to be able to decide things for
   himself
Just for once, have a good look at things and have a go at
   things
All by himself just for once, instead of never being able to
   turn around without asking for divine guidance, or take
   a step forward
Without leaning upon divine aid.
But it's not so. Man was ever so much happier before
His Father died.

He gets along pretty well as long as it's daylight; he works
   very hard,
And he amuses himself very hard with the many cunning
   amusements
This clever age affords.
But it's all no use; the moment it begins to get dark, as soon
   as it's night,
He goes out and howls over the grave of God.
It comes down to this: he wants to die too, he wants to be
   nothing.
And the next best thing to being nothing
Is being nobody."

*   *   *

95

MERTON
(*to Carl*)

Your violence offends me. Your sneering, supercilious
    bravado
Offends me. Your brutality and your vituperation
Offend me.

It is not love of the oppressed or even concern for them,
But hatred of the oppressor, that motivates your movements.

No empire is more thirsty for its conquest
Than you for yours.

And your recurrent dream
Is not of happy millions singing under a just régime,
But of happy millions killing, smashing furniture and de-
    filing floors.

CARL

Love and hate have nothing whatever to do with it. It is a
    simple matter
Of economics.
Therefore you do not see it, and you never can.
You are incapable of considering even for a moment what is
    against your interests. No man
Is good at this; but you are incapable of it. The factories
    belong
To you; and how does it happen that they belong to you?
    Because
You *own* them; and how does it happen that you own them?
    Because
You *built* them; and with what did you build them? With
    money which the laws

Of your country, which you passed, devoutly maintain
Belongs to *you!*

PYGMALION

Oh, God, must we go over that again?

Carl, I bet you ten dollars you can't keep your mouth shut
Ten minutes.

CARL

That so? I bet you ten cents I can.

PYGMALION

What time is it, Dick?

LUCAS

It's exactly twelve o'clock. It's neither *P.M.* nor *A.M.* it's
exactly *M.*

MERTON

Midnight. Midnight in New York. It will be almost dawn now
In Paris.

JOHN

I fear not, friend; I fear that in Paris, too,
It is midnight. Midnight in London; midnight in Madrid.
The whole round world rolling in darkness, as if it feared an
air-raid.
Not a mortal soul that can see his hand before his face.

PYGMALION

I bet you Mussolini gets the outline of his own iron glove
Even in the dark, damn well. And the outstretched paw
Of Hitler is a handsome blob of white to him
No matter what time it is.

Dick, you're not bad, for a wop.
But I don't care for Two-Gun Benito.

RICARDO

Benitissimo

To you. At least for the moment.

PYGMALION

Can't somebody stop
The son-of-a-wolf? What about appealing to his better
nature? Dick, why don't you?

RICARDO

He doesn't amuse me sufficiently. It *would* be,
However, a charming thing to do.

LUCAS

Gee, 'twould be fun
To tie him and Hitler together by their tails and hang them
over a clothes-line. . . .

RICARDO

Hitler is different . . . he's a pale, moustachioed soda-fountain
Siegfried; but he's a sort of Siegfried.
It's tiresome—but heroic—what Germany has done.

LUCAS
(*to Ricardo*)

Do you care enough about *anything* to fight for it?

RICARDO

I care a great deal about
One or two things; but I very much doubt
If I'd fight for them. I'm really in favour of having the
human race wiped out.

JOHN

But it won't be, Dick! The cheap will wipe out the fine,
That's all; and the race will continue.

PYGMALION

And be ruled by a brain like mine.

JOHN

A minor calamity only, not a true disaster.

PYGMALION

Don't be foolish, it's catastrophe. And it's coming. If you
want to outthink the thoughtless, you'll have to think
faster.

MERTON

London. Midnight in London . . . I don't like the English.
Our house is always full of them. My wife is one of those
women who fall
For the pipe-smoking, blue-eyed bastards, with that elegant
manner and no manners at all.
I can dispense with England.

RICARDO

You don't know what you're talking about!
Those pea-brained snobs are not England! Why, the whole
world
Cracks up, if England's wiped out!

MERTON

It's a pretty bad business, all right, and God knows how it
will end. . . .
France still licking her wounds, and with sad eyes
Circling the horizon: on no frontier a friend.

JOHN

Licking her wounds?—My God! standing like an exhausted
    fox,
Courageous and frightened, surrounded by Germany, Italy
    and Spain!
The world is in the jaws of hounds! Christ! Let the equinox
Rip up the world! What we need is forty days of rain.

PYGMALION

Being out of love, and out of mood with loving,
I said, "These lovers lead a sickening life:
Sighing, beseeching, kissing, accusing, proving,
Till Church or State pronounce them man and wife;
Nagging and jeering, scheming, accusing, spying,
Till Legal Aid pronounce them no such thing;
Then on again, kissing, beseeching, sighing—
A dainty dish to set before the King!"

Seeking to enlarge my narrow life's horizon,
I turned my mind upon affairs of state:—
Allied at noon, by midnight mixing poison,
Slandering, scheming, spying, lying in wait—
I saw the Powers and their employments plain;
Picked up the 'phone and fell in love again.

LUCAS

Ten minutes past twelve!

PYGMALION

All right, Carl; you can open your mouth.
(*Carl does so, in a prodigious honest yawn. Everybody laughs.*)

100

PYGMALION

I suppose you've been dying to do that for precisely the last
ten minutes.

CARL

I certainly have.

PYGMALION

Well, here's your ten bucks, Comrade.

CARL

Thanks.

RICARDO

Pygmalion, *you*? Have these ten minutes of boiling turned
you red?

PYGMALION

Not me.
With a firing-squad in every john, and a dictaphone
Under every bed!

CARL

Why, if you really are opposed to *anything* beyond personal
discomfort and loss of property,—*why*,
If you really are distressed by the prospect of another war,
Don't you do something about it?—all you do is wring your
hands and cry!
Why don't you consider by whom these wars are waged, and
what for?
Then fight all future war by fighting the fascist state?—
It is that, particularly, it seems to me, that you all hate.

MERTON

It is that among other things, not particularly, that we pro-
pose, if we cannot curb it, at least to isolate.

"War and Fascism" are not Siamese twins, in spite of your
  clever slogan. Imagine, if you can,
What will happen when Russia, whose birth-rate is rapidly
  increasing, becomes as crowded as Japan.

*   *   *

CARL
(to Merton)

Even on your own terms, even with everything your own
  way, you've made a mess of things.
You can't any longer even support your slaves in the slavery
To which they are accustomed. You are unfit to rule.

Your economics is a make-shift, hit-or-miss-assembled, third-
  degree, defensive war, offensive peace,
Stuffed eagle, eye for a tooth, compulsory school,
Lynch-law, plate-glass, red-plush, chromium, hennaed horse-
  hair,
Cellophane-wrapped what-not; a hand-to-mouth—
Septic-hand-to-sterilized-mouth affair.
It belongs in a side-show, along with all the other obese
Two-headed monstrosities. And don't worry, it will soon be
  there.

RICARDO

It is a pity these communists feel called upon to imbibe not
  only their morals
But also their manners, from Marx;
The grandfather of present-day communism regrettably has
  stamped his progeny
Not only (and this only on occasion) with the broad philo-
  sophical brow,

But also with the narrow humourless vanity and the shrill
    spite
That marred somewhat his articulation then as now.

He was a talented, intolerant, jealous, nasty old man.

It was the essential vulgarity of his mind that at length be-
    trayed him,
Despite his abstruse and admirable works into the arms of
    the vulgar.
Arrogance, abuse, bad temper, jealousy, spleen,
Are medicines easy for the mob to swallow, no capsules
Are required to disguise these tastes, they are licked from
    the spoon.

Few people, comparatively speaking, have read *Das Kapital*;
    those who say they have read it
Include, among others, earnest workers, who earnestly intend
To read it, but who, of course, work hard and have not the
    time.

I, who have infinite leisure to read, being a rich man
Uninterested in becoming any richer, and interested in books,
Have read it. It is a fascinating and a repulsive work;
Interminable, never for a moment brilliant, often profound,
Profound for pages, then suddenly infantile; best
When coldest, when most detached; it is a great work,
    truly,
But marred by jealousies, by hatred of a class which should
    have been—
By an economist, by a philosopher—considered only as one
Phenomenon in an anachronistic system about to fall.

CARL

And having said that, what, precisely, have you said?
You've informed us that you've read ·
Das Kapital, and that according to you Marx was talking
    through his whiskers; O. K.
Never mind how he said it; the point is: what did he *say*?
And speaking of "vulgarity," isn't it just a little bit cheap
To set the flaws of a great work—and you admit it to be a
    great work—in the front window; and try to keep
Its greatness in the back-lot?

RICARDO

I was using the word "vulgar" in the Latin sense.

CARL

You most decidedly were not.

MERTON
(*to Carl*)

Oppressed you *may* be, overworked or unemployed you *may*
    be,
But your Cause has been nursed and fostered in the generous
    lap
Of a liberal capitalistic state; you're an incubator baby,
Too weak to live in a draught, and accepting your pap
As your rightful due, and yelling for more, and not even a
    thank-you
To the system to which you owe your life, and which you
    mean to destroy
The moment you can stand on your feet! By God, *I'd* yank
    you
Out into the world—and you wouldn't have a printing-press
    for a toy

Either, or a nation-wide hook-up for a red tin horn,
If I had my say-so! But the government's a soft old fool,
Always getting all het up about the prematurely born,
And spending millions to cart a lot of queer-shaped heads to
    school.
You're pretty well off, I can tell you, in the U. S. A.
Think of me, when you're feeling homesick for the good old
    times some day.

CARL

Don't worry, there'll be plenty of people thinking of you
When the moment's ripe. You might even get a post-card
    saying, "Dear
Merton, Cross marks modest apartment in the new
State Penitentiary. Wishing you were here."

MERTON

Why, that's no news! Do you think I don't know that?
That's what I've been saying all along. Do you think I don't
    know
That with *you* in power I wouldn't stand the chance of a rat
In a research laboratory?—Yet here you come and go
Unmolested, and shoot off your mouth, and publish the
    Daily Worker, and insist
On your rights under a liberal Constitution! Tell me, would
    you care
To try publishing in Moscow today a paper called the Daily
    Capitalist?
Or preach the blessings of the profit-system to a crowd in
    the Red Square?

CARL

That's a quite different matter. Look here, even to your
    warped vision isn't it plain

That there's a difference between overthrowing a tyrannical
government that is oppressing the majority of the
people,
And scheming to undermine a government of the people for
private gain?

MERTON

Certainly there's a difference. But suppose it were my
honest conviction
That society from the bottom up is better off when divided
into classes?
Suppose it were my impartial judgment that the amount of
enslavement and affliction
Among the poor is less in a capitalist state than under a dic-
tator-for-life chosen by the masses?
Should I be allowed to express that point of view or not?

CARL

In the first place, you'd be crazy . . .!

PYGMALION

And in the second place, you'd be shot.

RICARDO

Don't let it excite you, Merton. By the time we get communism here,
It will have grown so bourgeois that you'll hardly notice the
difference. Tammany Hall has already begun to appear
In Russia. Give a Comrade the chance
To hand out jobs, and he hands them to the boys from the
home town, and to his sisters and his cousins and his
aunts.

CARL

All that's being changed!

RICARDO

Things have been changed here, too,
When under pressure it seemed the expedient thing to do.

MERTON
(to Carl)

In order to build new factories, in order even
To putty new window-panes into cobwebbed factory-
   windows, in order to repair
Old machinery, to say nothing of buying new; in order to
   procure
The raw materials of production; in order to be free to drill
The well that may not gush; to plant the acres that may be
   scorched or drowned
Before the season of the harvest; in order to risk great loss,
   and even in the good times
To wait for years before the enterprise begins to pay even
   its initial cost,—
You must have capital.
Your proletarian state will be a proletarian state only in the
   morning,
While it labours for its daily bread and shelter and shoes;
In the afternoon, that state will become a capitalist
Or it will cease to exist.

The surplus value that today, unjustly or justly,
Is taken over by the individual factory-owner to re-invest
In implements and materials, or to speculate with, or to
   fritter away,
Will be seized by the State, less adroitly but more ruthlessly
   even,
To be dispensed as the State sees fit, for sound or injudicious
   purchasing,

For uniforms, for statues, for obsolete or unproven and impracticable machinery, or for efficient machinery;
For war, or for peace,—probably for both, as is the case
today.
The worker will be quite as helpless then as now: he will
earn a living of sorts, and the rest will go to his em-
ployer, that is, the State, and he will have nothing to
say.

Carl

Don't worry, we can work it out, we're quite as brainy as you,
And we've no mental alimony to pay to an incompatible
Ideal!—
That saps a man's resources.
                              A class that must daily construe
Its evil deeds in terms of righteousness has a part-time job
to do
That will eventually exhaust it for the day.

                              The class that need not conceal
Either from the world or from itself what is its real
Objective, proceeds at once from the will to the deed, with
no terrain
Of hilly evasion and swampy compromise to cross before it
gain
Its goal.
Split men go forth to war in vain
Against the undivided. The flawed cannot defeat the whole.

Merton

Interesting, of course, if true; but if true, then as true
Of the Hitlerite, and of the termite, as of you.

Ricardo

If, however, singleness of purpose and direct approach could
    contend
With deviousness and guile, we should not be here, my
    friend.
Sealed in Jurassic mortar the just bones repose
Of many a race that knew what it wanted and followed its
    nose.

Carl

Precisely. And today it's the capitalistic system that's so
    over-weight it can hardly waddle.
                If you have tears
For a prehistoric monster prepare to shed them now, for it's
    about to croak.
Oh, it can feed itself still by grabbing everything in reach
    for another few years
Perhaps; but there are conditions under which to be a stick-
    in-the-mud ceases to be a joke.

Merton

The fittest to survive may well derive some satisfaction,
But should refrain from finding cause for pride, in that:
The value of a life is not determined by that life's protraction:
The fittest to survive in a sewer, is a sewer-rat.

Pygmalion
(*as if to himself*)

The world stinks. It stinks like a dead cat under a door-
    step. It stinks to hell.
Wherever I step I have to hold my nose, the world stinks so.
I can't get to windward of the stink, there's not a breath of
    air
Stirring, just a big stink squatting under the hot sky.

Pyg, you're drunk.

PYGMALION

You bet I'm drunk. Do you think I don't know
Which side my gin is bittered on? Have you had a good
whiff
Of this stinking world, and still you want to stay sober?

RICARDO

If you do not believe in God it is a good thing
To believe in Communism. There is much comfort,
As I observe, when lowering into an oblong hole a much
prized object,
In the reflection that it is either (a) safe in the arms of
Jesus, or (b)
Only a cog in a wheel and that the wheel continues to re-
volve and that that is the important thing.

If you do not believe in God and cannot bring yourself
To believe in Communism, then, I may say, you are in a
singularly
Unprotected position.
You have not so much as a last year's mullein-stalk to set
your back against; all winds blow upon you.

As for myself, I do not believe in God and I do not care for
The society of people.

I am willing to give them my coat, but I am not willing
To lend them my coat and have them wear it and return it.
I am willing to give them my loaf, but I am not willing
To sit and share it with them.
I do not wish to die, but I would rather die

Than have for my daily horizon year in-year out—and sing
    Huzza! into the bargain—
The hairs on the backs of the necks of other people.
And I would rather stand with my back against an icy,
    unintelligible void
Than be steamed upon from behind by the honest breaths of
    many well-wishers.

CARL

Ricardo, Ricardo, wilt thou be mine?
Thou shalt not wash dishes, nor yet feed the swine;
But sit on a fence, and sew a fine seam,
And feed upon Communists, Christians and cream!
Oh, it's all very well for you, you silk-lined Liberal—
I'm wrong, Anselmo's wrong, Pygmalion's wrong,
You're right; but who the hell are you, and even if you were
    somebody,
What's your program? You haven't any program. You say,
"Tut, tut, it's all very bad, it's all very awkward,
It's extremely unpleasant; it's even somewhat painful.
God's gone fishing. All's wrong with the world. Tut, tut."

RICARDO

If I'm sitting on a fence, it's a barbed-wire fence, and it
    hurts me
More than it does you.

CARL

You talk too well.
And you talk too god-damned much.
What about an adolescent stutter, just for a change,
And a sturdy, inarticulate GOOD IDEA?

III

RICARDO

It is difficult to dramatize the liberal attitude; therefore we
    have no following. Our flag,
Unless it flap at half-mast, floats too high
For the crude of vision to perceive.
We weave
No pattern of uniformed men in the shape of our emblem;
    we sing no lusty song; we have no battle-cry.
Bright colour and insistent noise attract
The multitude, without whose perilous favour
We may exist, but cannot act.
The simple man wants food, and wants to fight and sing.
How shall the thoughtful, the unshouted thing
Prevail with him? Though it should feed him better than
    ever he was fed before,
Offering no outlet for his intense but simple spirit's need, no
    marching,
Monotonous, . . . hypnotic; no dances easy to learn;
It offers him food, and nothing more.

Only by self-defilement could a liberal party earn
A place among the branded herds; and to return
From shoddy years, from Avernus, is not easy.
Caught
In the amorphous amber of vulgarity would sit at length,
Helpless and fossilized, the winged, the noble thought.
Vulgarity alone has strength.

JOHN

If that were true,
Ricardo—and you will bear with me, for I am quoting you—
We should not now be here.
Not through the headlong, indiscriminate advance

Of unicellular minds, nor yet through the adroit
Juxtapositions of sardonic Chance
Do those great miracles appear
Which all men use, and better their condition by; and though
they are unaware
To what extent superior is that egregious force, or with char-
acteristic debonair
Assurance give it no thought at all, yet the egregious force
is there,—
Feeding the herd that otherwise would go,
Starving, in search of grass in exhausted pastures where it
has ceased to grow.
The liberal, the deliberate, the low of voice
Might well adopt by choice
And charter what is their fitting and historic rôle:
These are the whisperers-together, these from all time
Have been the angelic spies in the loud councils of the con-
fident lost,
The insidious lobby, plausibly in terms of saving and cost
Planting the untemporal seed; the insistent leaven
That leavens the reluctant whole.

Pygmalion
(aloud, but to himself)

The world's so full of sons-of-bitches it makes me feel down-
right conspicuous: sons-of-bitches having roses
Named after them; sons-of-bitches endowing charities; sons-
of-bitches begging for alms;
Sons-of-bitches at Tropical putting sponges up the horses'
noses;
And sons-of-bitches at Hialeah hacking their initials in the
royal palms.

JOHN

Pyg, is that a fighting-jag or a weeping-jag you've got?

PYGMALION

It's neither. I'm afraid I'm going to sing. I hope not.
I'll be sick if I do.

JOHN AND LUCAS
(*together*)

Me, too.

CARL

Old men, you are dying!
Winter will find you scattered like sparrows over the snow;
Neat little sparrows, folded and stiff on the snow.

We will sweep you up with tender brooms,
For your song, although monotonous, was sweet:
"Plenty to eat!" you sang; "Plenty to eat!"

Guard your health; preserve your powers;
Today is yours. But tomorrow is ours.

PYGMALION

That's what *you* think—and who the hell cares what *you*
    think?
In the first place, you *mayn't* think, because you're not
    allowed to think;
And in the second place, you couldn't think even if you were
    allowed to, your head's
So full of dope, so full of happy-dust, so full of snuffed-up
Proletarian happy-dust.
You, an intellectual? You? Dream on; you're just a drug
Addict.

MERTON
(to Carl)

You stand for the death of everything I care for.
God, we've spent years proving that the world is round!—
And you'd make it flat again!

There's not a mountain left in Russia—you've flattened
    them all out,
With your shoulder-to-shoulder, community-singing, tramp-
    tramp-tramp.
There's not a mountain left in Germany or in Italy, either—
All three flattened out, as flat as pan-cakes—the pan-cakes
    of Europe.

If you had your way, we'd live in a two-dimensional world,
All dutifully munching mulberry-leaves for the State.
Every man for the State, and the devil take the individual.

Horrible, this levelling of peaks; obscene, this promiscuity.
Insects, that's what you are—a colony of ants.

Yes, and it won't work, either; you'd much better stick to
    being men, and improve your condition
With your exclusively human characteristics in mind. This
    community stuff, I grant, is
As a means to an end, effective; but it offers no future;
    there's too much competition:
A man will never be such a good ant as an ant is.

RICARDO

All soil is rock under the wafted seed of Reason;
Wherever it falls, it falls on stony ground.

Sentiment, jealousy, cruelty, anger, fear
Tap at the door of the mind and are admitted at once;
But Reason knocks in vain at that occupied ear;
It has no appointment, and the mind is in conference.

The End might justify the Means, if the End could stand
Pure of the Means, but it cannot, it is for ever polluted;
Its ear is whispered in, it nods, it smiles,
It puts on fat, it abdicates,—and the Means
Assumes its radiant crown.
Stalin is the Means
Seated in the throne of the End.

MERTON

Oh, God, why live, to breathe a prescribed and rationed air!
    —All free
Opinion, all interchange of vigorous thought, suffocated
By the poisonous motor-exhaust of motor minds!
Passion regimented; curiosity regimented; endeavour regi-
    mented;
Culture, and grace, and all the things I cared for
Equally divided among the mob, and sauced to their taste!
This is the time for the proud to take his pride by the hilt
And slit his bowels with it; this is the time for the individual,
    for me,
To lock himself in his room . . . and get it over with.

CARL
(to Merton)

You, an individual?—you, you regimented mouse?
You Harvard Club, Union Club, white tie for the opera,
    black tie for the theatre,
Trouser legs a little wider this year, sir,

I would suggest dark blue instead of black, sir,
Pumps are no longer worn, sir,
Mah-Johnng, cross-word, anagram, backgammon, whist,
    bridge, auction, contract, regimented mouse!
Why, you're so accustomed to being flanked to right and left
    by people just like yourself
That if they ever *should* step aside you couldn't stand up!

No, that's the least of your troubles, my beamish boy.
We know what you'd shinny up a tree with if the jabberwocky
    came—
Unless it was too heavy to climb with, in which case you'd
Stay on the ground tugging at it until you were clawed to
    death.

The trouble is, you are regimented to no purpose:
Millions of you in your golf-stockings goose-stepping nowhere.

You, an individual?
You salad for luncheon, soup for dinner,
Maine for summer, Florida for winter,
Wife-pampering dog-worshipper!

"Mertie, I believe I left my knitting in the living-room."
(*Well, what the hell's that to me?—are you paralyzed?*) You
    don't say it, though.
"Mertie, we're having dinner tonight with the Doolittle-
    Doolesses."
(*Like hell we are!*) You are, though.

"Damn it all, has that dog of yours got to have the only
    chair in the room where there's a light you can read
    by?"

Answer is, yes.

Knit, knit,
Read in the dark.
House full of dogs'-chairs,
Cadillac full of dogs'-hairs.

"Mertie, don't you think you ought to take the dogs out?"

Millions of you taking the dogs out, standing respectfully
Waiting, while they mess up the sidewalks.

Oh, sweet, mild night!—Park Avenue deserted, and the
    moon shining down
On all the little dog-heaps.

MERTON
(to Carl)

Your masses are fleas, not men; this vaunted exodus
From increasingly unbearable conditions is but the natural
    scurrying away
From the dying body of the present economic system: hop
    in what direction you may,
You are parasites all;
Without your host of a superior organism you cannot exist.
If you're not cracked between two thumb-nails before fall
I'll meet you at the flea circus,
Pumping supper from a sanguine Georgian wrist.

CARL

By God! You! Leviathan!—with your poisonous flesh that
    not even a crab would touch, and your belly fat
With a million minnows, can sit there and say that!

MERTON

A million shrimps!

RICARDO

Gentlemen! Gentlemen!

PYGMALION

Atta boy,
Mertie! Atta boy, Carl! Keep out of this, Dick! Don't be so
god-damned
Refined! Let 'em scrap it out! Come on, all hands:
Let's take up the rugs before the crimson pool expands!

RICARDO

Lucas, come here and hold their noses, while I pour
The brigands full of Scotch! Here, Merton,—drink this like
a man—a little Christmas spirit, that's all; the argument's closed.
Carl, drown yourself in this, and have pity upon a nervous
host, opposed
Not only to fascism, but also to war.

MERTON

Nobody need hold my nose. Where'd this come from? I
didn't know you had anything in the house to drink.
Besides, mine's Bourbon.

RICARDO

Was Bourbon; and will be again as soon as I fetch another
bottle. In the meantime, take this.

PYGMALION

I think
You're being partial, and I think it's just no fair, and I
thought we were pals!

RICARDO

You,—you're soused already to the semi-circular canals!
Crawl over here and help yourself.

PYGMALION

Have you heard the one about—?

RICARDO

Yes! And so has everybody else!

PYGMALION

I don't think you meant to shout,
Richard, but you were *shout*ing. What I was willing to do,
And solely to entertain you, was to tell you about the
young lady from Kew.

RICARDO

I've heard it.

PYGMALION

Dick, may Lucas play
Something *irreverent* on that solemn Steinway?
Oh, *Dick!* Do you dance the tango?

RICARDO

Yes. But not with you.
Play something, Lucas.

LUCAS
(*at the piano*)

What shall I play?

PYGMALION

That little thing
From *Faust*, that goes like this . . .

JOHN

Play something nobody can sing.

MERTON

Play *Home, Sweet Home*; I've got to be getting out of here.
Worst dive in town. And no bouncer to throw the elderly
    nuisance out on his ear.
Grand night, Ricardo, grand. Wish I could tell
Just why I love coming down here and getting beaten up so
    well.

PYGMALION

Lucas, *don't* play that! *Don't!* It breaks my heart!
It reminds me of winter in Vienna!—and the sweetest little
    tart
You ever took shopping for galoshes . . . Dick!
When does this party start?

*   *   *

"Sorry to have kept you waiting for me, Frank,"
Said Merton to his chauffeur. "If I had known—"

"Oh, that's all right, sir."

           "Is that my cigarette-case? Thank
You, John, where'd you find it?"

           "Well, I found it, along with my own,
In my left breast-pocket."

           "I'm damned! Were you drunk?"

           "Oh, well,
I wouldn't say that; afloat, maybe, not adrift."

"You going uptown, Carl?"

　　　　　　　"Thanks, I'm taking the L;
It brings me within a block of my door."

　　　　　　　"Can I give you a lift,
Lucas?"

"Why, yes, if you're sure it won't put you out."

"Get in! . . . Good-night!"

　　　　　　　"Good-night!"

　　　　　　　"Say, what do you say
We go 'round to Tony's and see who's there?"

　　　　　　　　　"I doubt
If he's open; it's after two."

　　　　　　　"You going my way,
John? let's walk; there's not a taxi in sight."

"Good-night, Ricardo!"

　　　　　　"Happy dreams!"

　　　　　　　　"Good-night!"

THE END

TABLE OF FIRST LINES

Part I

PART II